AQUAPONICS

Simple Guide to Growing Vegetables Using
Aquaponics

(A Step by Step Aquaponics Gardening Guide for
Growing Vegetables)

Robert Hargrove

Published By Tyson Maxwell

Robert Hargrove

All Rights Reserved

Aquaponics: Simple Guide to Growing Vegetables Using Aquaponics (A Step by Step Aquaponics Gardening Guide for Growing Vegetables)

ISBN 978-1-77485-262-0

Legal & Disclaimer

Table of Contents

Introduction

Aquaponics is an excellent method to raise fish and other food items in a single space, however the main problem for many people is how to make it work. Since a lot of plants do well in aquaponics, it's easy to become overwhelmed and want to cultivate every single thing! If you have the right setup it's possible to do this but it'll be more difficult to grow healthy plants if your a novice, so it's a great suggestion to start with a with a small. In the same way, even if selected plants that are already growing in a way that is suitable for your space, it could be the most difficult task.

An aquaponic setup could be as simple as an aquarium with fish in it and a pot over it, however this isn't very effective. If you're confident with the basic concepts of aquaponics then this is the perfect guide to figure out the best method to make the most of your space and cultivate any plants you'd like to.

The main thing you need to consider when setting up an effective aquaponic setup is

1

to make sure that your plants are getting their three primary needs met that is water, light and nutrients. Since nutrients and water are both the same thing, it means that the growing area must be sufficiently flooded or the plants will fail to thrive. Too much water is, however could cause them to rot. If you're not familiar with the basics of aquaponics laying down, the road ahead of the game. This is an intermediate guide to those already acquainted with the basics of how aquaponics operates.

If you're looking for plants to start, you'll have to either source plants that have already been grown in a hydroponic system or grow them yourself using seeds. Aquaponics seeding isn't that difficult. It's best to begin them with an organic material such as rock wool or coir since they're small and won't split to enable the root system to grow while giving the support that the roots require. It's not recommended to move plants out of soil as there is an extremely high risk of shock. In the same way, transferring plants out of soil can mean there is a risk of introducing the bacteria and other contaminants that can impact your fish. Aquaponic systems are delicate and requires to be kept in check, in both the interest of the health of the fish as well as plants.

For your plants to flourish, it is sometimes necessary to be a bit creative. It's not about better equipment, but rather being more creative with the tools you've got or have access to!

What we'll explore is some innovative methods to increase the size of your plants, and address the most common issues that confront many growers to ensure that your plants are the best they canbe!

Chapter 1: What Is Aquaponics?

Aquaponics is basically a method where plants and fish collaborate to ensure that both thrive. Both are nurtured through the system that is built to make use of the recirculation process of its biological processes. This system of ecological design involves the an excess of waste produced by the fish, which is then treated by bacteria before being transformed to produce plant food that is then used to cleanse the water for fish. Each of them plays a role within the Aquaponics system, which allows people to access a wealth of sustainable, healthy fresh food sources from both fish and vegetation. The system was developed out of the combination of the best aspects that comprise Hydroponics and aquaculture all while eliminating the negatives that come with both, including fertilizer additives made of chemicals as well as the necessity of dumping water, as well as filtration.

History and current uses

Aquaponics might be growing in popularity and usage among commercial farmers and home-grown growers however it's not a brand new idea. We just have the privilege of using the latest and upgraded, as well as much simpler methods of Aquaponics. According to the saying, the past repeats itself, and those who are smart are able to learn from those who came before us. It is never going to stop me from marveling at how long ago, prior to the invention of technology, before machines as well as mass communication and social media, our forefathers were able to come up with such amazing inventions that enabled them to only survive , but flourish in many locations where the environment was believed to be the biggest obstacle.

In a variety of forms or, Aquaponics was used throughout the continent, in areas such as China's rice paddy fields and in Africa and in Italy and throughout the islands as well as through Native Americans, and the Aztecs in Mexico for example, just to mention several. The Aztecs moved to the area now known in the present as Mexico City. The area did not have the best soil for agriculture, and the interior areas were mostly marshy. To adjust to the conditions of this inefficient environment They built numerous floating rafts around the lake, made of materials found in the region, like reeds and mud. On the rafts, they built gardens that made use of the nutrients of the aquatic species found in the lake to feed the plants.

In the past, when people lived off the land (in certain places there are still people who live off the land) it was crucial to be aware of nature, observe the natural process of nature and utilize it in all areas of life. In light of the observations made, we now have Aquaponics now! It is important to remember that third world nations - as the Aztecs long ago had to contend with challenges in their environments, such as poor soil, insufficient water, and a lot of people were hungry. Numerous organizations are now stepping up and introduce Aquaponics due to their speedy food expansion without much water or soil-free gardening abilities. Apart from being a crucial nutritional source of food, the system provides healthy, healthier eating and essential vitamins and nutrients that assist in strengthening the immune system and fighting illnesses. It also helps to stop the spread of illnesses in one area of the globe, it also stops the spread of illness across the globe!

Chapter 2: Types Of Aquaponics Systems

There are a variety of systems utilized in setting an aquaponics plant. Some of the most well-known systems used by the majority homeowners are the beds that are filled with media as well as the NFT (nutrient film technique) and DWC (deep water cultivation).

Media Filled Beds

These are the most basic and most widely used aquaponics system. They are filled and cleaned with rock, including expanded clay as well as other similar substances. Plants can be cultivated in this kind of medium. A pump is employed to transport water out of the tank in which fishes are raised to media beds. Water flows either in a continuous stream over the rocks or flows into the beds of media, which is then removed after a time.

For systems that use flood drain cycle the process can be completed by a variety of methods. There are three primary methods to be accomplished: using the timed pump, an auto-siphon or simple standpipes.

Certain beds that are filled with media use the use of a timer. It decides when to fill the beds with water from the tank by activating the pump, and when it's time to remove it by turning off the water pump. A standpipe is installed in the growing beds to limit the amount of water that floods them.

The process of draining and flooding the grow beds can be done by using an auto siphon

The beds are placed in the beds, the pump can be running continuously. The siphon will take the water out of the grow beds and then return them to the fish tank.

A bedpipe as well as a pump that runs continuously is another way to drain and flood.

Pros and Pros and

This article focuses on the advantages and disadvantages of this method of aquaponics.

Pros

This system is ideal for those who have taken to aquaponics as a pastime.

The parts needed to run the system are readily available. They don't cost excessively also. It is possible to get the material easily.

The dimensions of the device will depend on the type of interest you have. It is possible to make it either a large or small one. It will allow you to conserve a significant amount of space with this technique.

You will be able to cultivate a variety of plants.

-

Cons

This system must be maintained on a frequent on a regular

There could be some areas within the whole system that are now anaerobic.

Nutrient Film Technique (NFT)

This method is typically used in hydroponics however it also is useful in aquaponics. In NFT the water containing the nutrients (from tank fish) is then pumped into plants via small drains. These gutters are sealed and the water is pumped through it in thin films. The plants are placed in tiny plastic cups, and their roots have access to the films of water to absorb nutrients.

This technique is not recommended for specific plants. Green plants like the leafy variety would flourish with NFT. The plants that are too big for plastic cups or with massive and extensive root systems aren't recommended for this type of system. The plants that are too big to be hanged within plastic cup are not recommended for the NFT.

Pros and Pros and

This section outlines the advantages and disadvantages of this method of aquaponics.

Pros

The materials used that make up this system are easily accessible. There are parts that make up this system on the marketplace with ease.

The conditions for growing this method are more specific. It is possible to choose your plants easily.

You'll find that it is possible to change the media with no needing to be concerned about changing the acidity of your water. Any change in pH could be extremely hazardous for the plants within the system.

Cons

It is necessary to purify the water regularly. It is essential to do this correctly. It is likely that the fish are dying otherwise. It is impossible to grow a large number of crops within this particular system. This is due to the requirements created through the program.

Deep Water Culture

The system works with the plant floating over the surface while the roots hang from the water. It is among the most widely used aquaponics techniques to grow commercially. There are a variety of methods to accomplish this. Certain growers put their plants on foam rafts and let them flounder through a tank which is constantly full of liquid from the aquarium. The water is continuously cycled through the plant and back down into the tank.

Chift Pist System

It is among the most well-known DIY aquaponics methods. Sump tanks house water, which is then pumped into the tank, where the fish live. When the water is being pumped into the tank, the level of water increases until it is overflowing. The excess water drains from the aquarium to the growing beds. The water that enters the beds of grow eventually disappears in the sump tank. A self-siphon is installed within the bed of the garden to limit the drainage and flooding.

In many cases, growers use an SLO into the Chift Pist System. SLO stands for Solids Lift Overflow. A pipe for overflow is fitted in the fish tank which is then lowered to the bottom of the tank. It will then draw all the solids (i.e. the waste of fish) which settle at the bottom of the tank and then move it into growing beds.

There are numerous advantages for this method. One advantage lies in the fact that it is far from the waste and fish. It is situated in the tank that is used for sump. In this way, the pump will function better without causing disturbance to the fish and agitating wastes which could cause water to become cloudy. This system also ensures a consistent levels of the water in the fish tank, which decreases the stress on the fish. It is also suggested method for large fish tanks since it improves the circulation of water and the removal of waste more effective.

There are some disadvantages with the chift system. There is the requirement to set up additional equipment such as also known as the sump tank. In order to make this work the fish tank or stand needs to be tall. In addition, this method will require a larger space for the whole installation. Timers are not a possibility to utilize for this setup.

Aquaponics systems are as simple depending on the preferences of the grower. The easiest way to begin and especially for those who don't need to buy equipment is to create an aquarium that is a normal one. Pick up a few pieces polystyrene. Make a few tiny holes into it. Put cuttings of plants like mint and watercress in these holes. Place the polystyrene pieces on the surface of the water. Set up fish and within a matter of minutes it's a simple aquaponics setup.

Based on decades of study and feedback, the majority of aquaponics gardeners see the flooding and drain system as the simplest and most robust among all the systems. The system needs a minimum amount of upkeep and maintenance. It is also the most suggested system for those who are just starting out.

Chapter 3: Designing A System

Making an aquaponics setup can be simple if you know how to construct an aquaponics system in the correct method the first time. An easy, but efficient system doesn't have to cost a lot of money and can be constructed with simple tools and easy to locate materials. Here are some of the basic steps to follow when the common system is built.

The most popular type of aquaponics system is built around two major pieces of equipment. This is usually a tank to house the fish, and an in-situ tank or growing bed for the plants. There are tanks specifically designed specifically for this purpose, but it is common to find DIY tanks or large containers that work perfectly, and might cost less.

The fish tank may be an aquarium, or any other large container that can contain water and is constructed out of non-toxic materials. It is usually located near to the ground. The tank used for plants is typically placed over an aquarium for fish.

This is not only a way to keep the plants at a suitable setting for them to work from and also makes plumbing more efficient, allowing water to flow back to the tank through gravity.

You'll require an water pump as well as a pipe or hose to move water from the tank into the growing tank. A return pipe lets water return to in the aquarium. The pipe must be placed at the right level inside the grow tank, so that the water can flow into it, while keeping the correct level of water. It is crucial that oxygen is delivered to the water. This can be achieved by using an air pump or air stone. The return pipe could be designed to pull air into the water while it drains the tank. An aquaponics book will show you how to build this. A battery-powered emergency air supply system recommended in the event of main pump or power failure.

The next step is to choose if you would like to use a growing medium such as clay pellets or gravel for your plants to grow in, or floating rafts. There are pros and cons for both. The floating one is affordable, simple, light and more convenient to move. Growing mediums can offer more secure anchors for larger plants . They provide a wonderful environment for the bacteria to flourish that help transform the waste of fish into plants' nutrients. A quality guide to aquaponics will be able to assist you determine what is most suitable for your needs.

Aquaponics is an excellent method to cultivate organic and fresh fish and vegetables. Many commercial and home gardeners as also farmers are seeing amazing outcomes with these systems.

How to construct an aquaponics destop

A mini aquaponics system is the ideal method of demonstrating aquaponic concepts and the nitrification process in a recirculating water environment. Here are the steps to build an inexpensive system that's ideal for teachers or student who are looking to start their journey in aquaponics. If you're seeking a complete set take a look out our Clear Flow aquaponic Systems(r)

What You'll Have to

Below is a list of the components you'll require to create an aquaponic miniature system. In the next part, Component Explaination, describes and the various components and offers suggestions for alternate items as well as specific products.

A tank for fish: 3 to 20 gallon glass or plastic containers ($5 between $20 and $5)

The gravel: 2.5 lbs. of gravel per 5 gallons of water that is in the tank for fish ($2 $5)

Pump for water: 3- 4 Watts with the capacity to lift up 18" to 54" with a capacity of 30 to 100 gallons/hour (small circulator or fountain pumps are best) ($19 to $40)

3 feet. of tubing made from plastic which fits into the outlet of your water pump. ($1 $ - $2)

Aquarium air pumps are sized to the quantity of gallons of your tank ($8 between $16 and $8)

The air stone (1" 1" -") ($1 $ - $2)

3 feet. in air tube to link the air stone to the pump (must be able to fit into the outlet of the air pump) ($1)

Grow Bed: It must be placed on top of the tank. It must also be three" to 8" deep ($5 to $20)

Growing Medium: sufficient perlite, pea gravel, coconut Coir clay pebbles that have been expanded or peat moss for the bed of growing ($2 between $5 and $2)

pH test kit, and dependent upon the pH level of your drinking water, either pH up or up ($5 between $5 and $15)

Plants and fish

Tools Essential

Drill using 1/8" or 3/16" bit and 1/2" bit

Scissors

Electrical tape

Component Explanation

A tank to house the fish

The tank could be a glass or plexiglass aquarium, or any other container that is able to hold water: like an plastic bucket, tub or barrel. We suggest anything from 3 to 20 gallons however, you could choose a larger tank in case you have room. Small plastic amphibian cages that are clean that are available at most pet shops, can be an ideal mini-system. They can hold up to 3 gallons and are cheap.

The usual size fish aquariums between 10 and 20 gallons are also affordable. The bigger tank, the greater surface for growing you can accommodate. In general you can accommodate 1 to two square feet grow area for every 10 gallons aquarium water.

Gravel to fill the bottom of the tank

The gravel provides place for the nitrifying organisms which convert ammonia into Nitrite, and later to nitrate. Nitrate can be utilized by plants. Many pet stores stock an aquarium with natural or colored gravel. The pebbles themselves are around one eighth" by 1/8" in diameter. Make sure you wash the gravel well prior to using it since it's often dusty. The dirt that is not cleaned will contaminate the water in your tank.

Tubing and water pump

A water pump of a small size is used to transfer the water from the tank to the growing bed. Once the water has been transferred to the grow bed, it is then fed back into the fish tank. It is necessary to have enough tubing connect the outlet of the pump up to at the highest point of the growing bed and create a circular shape inside it.

Air pump tubing, air stone and air pump

It is necessary to have an air pump to pump air into the tank's water, for both fish and plants. The air pump is connected via tubing and an air stone that is located at on the floor of the tank. The air stone breaks up the flow of bubbles that are coming out of the pump tiny bubbles that greatly enhance the oxygen levels in the water.

Grow in bed

A grow bed which is situated on the tank's top, should be slightly bigger than the width and length of the tank. The beds are filled with growth medium for the plants to are able to grow in. Plastic Rubbermaid container or garden planter or another container that will be placed on the top of the tank will do the trick. The container should be 3" to eight" deep.

It is possible to use the tub made of plastic or, for a beautiful device, make one of plexi-glass , and then make it sealable with a non-toxic silicone glue. If you create your own grow beds, you could incorporate an aquarium light by creating a hollow within the grow bed which the light will slide into. If you're using other type of container it is possible to place a light behind it, provided there is enough space.

Medium for growth

Growing mediums are porous and chemically inert substance that supports the roots of the plant and holds the moisture. Examples include perlite, clay pebbles that have been expanded Peat moss, peat gravel, and coconut Coir. It is essential to have enough material to fill the bed of your growing bed.

Plants and fish

In an aquaponic system fish supply the plant with the nutrients they require and the plants cleanse the water through the consumption of the essential nutrients.

Optional Components

The heater for the aquarium (for the tropical fish)

The majority of aquarists or gardeners setting aquaponic systems choose ornamental fish for their tanks and the majority of ornamental fish come from out of tropical oceans. The temperature of the tank should be 78 degrees F is required to maintain for the tropical fish. Two types of heaters for aquariums are available either tank-side or submerged. Both are suitable however, make sure that the heater you select is appropriate for the amount in gallons that will be in the tank you have for your fish. If your aquaponics system is located within an environment where temperature of the air is kept between 70 and 76 degrees F or in the case of a cool water fish like goldfish there is no need for heater.

Light for the fish tank

A majority of aquariums have a fluorescent light, which allows you to view the fish and check their health. You can also add one if you'd like but it's not necessary.

Grow light for plants

If you have your aquarium in a location with poor lighting it is possible to supplement artificial light sources to ensure healthy growth of the plant. Be aware that bright lights will increase the growth of algae within the tank. It is recommended to direct an artificial light to ensure that it doesn't directly enter the tank. If you are experiencing an increase in algae it is possible to scrape the walls of your tank, or buy the plecostomus fish that consumes algae. If your garden is located in a window with light, or in a greenhouse, or with plants that require minimal light levels growing lights aren't required.

Assembly Instructions

Step 1

Clean the gravel thoroughly and put it in the aquarium's bottom.

Step 2

You should drill 1/8" or 3/16" holes into the base of your bed every two square inches so that the water will run off to the storage tank. On one of the corners in the back of the bed create one 1/2" hole that allows the tubing coming from the pump water to flow through.

Step 3.

Place the water pump into the fish tank, then place your grow beds on the top in the aquarium. The tubing is fed from the water pump into an 1/2" hole. Allow enough tubing to reach around 3/4 of the length of the bed for growing and wrap around the entire inside of the bed. Cut any excess tubing and fold it over. Secure the folded part by using electrical tape.

Step 4

The grow bed should be filled with the growing medium until just below the surface of the tube.

Step 5

Small holes should be punched every 2 inches within the section of tubing which loops into the grow bed.

Step 6

Wrap the tubing loop with one or two inches in growing medium.

Step 7

Fill the tank with water. Connect the pump to make sure that the water flows into the grow bed. It then drips down into the growing medium , and continues to flow back to the tank. Based on the size that your tank is, the grow beds and pumps, you might be required to adjust the flow.

Step 8

Connect your an airstone to your air pump via an air tube. Put the air stone inside the tank, then plug into your air compressor. The constant stream of bubbles will rise from the water, bringing fresh air.

Step 9

Verify for the level of pH in your pool with litmus paper and the pH test kit or pH meters. Limtmus paper and pH test kits are readily available at most hardware stores for pool supplies. The optimal pH should be 7.0 for aquaponic systems. If it's more than 7.2 you must lower it by using an "pH lower" product, and if it's lower than 6.8 you need to raise it by using an "pH up" product both of which can be purchased from the aquarium store.

Step 10

Let the unit sit for 24 hours so that you can be certain that the chlorine has gone out of the water. If you wish to start stocking your fish as soon as possible then you'll need to use chlorine remover. It is available at pet stores and aquarium shops.

Step 11

Include your fish in the tank for fish. In the beginning, you should add not more than 1" of fish in a gallon. Once your system is set up for more than a month you can increase your fish density up to one" each gallon.

Step 12

Ideally, you should wait around 4 weeks before adding plants to your plant system If you're determined to plant your garden you can add a few plants or seeds, and then increase the your plant population in a month or so after your system is established.

and Plant Selection. and Plant Selection

When selecting your fish, make sure you choose tough species such as angelfish, guppies, goldfish and other popular varieties that are available at your local pet store or aquarium. The majority of desktop aquaponic gardens do not have fish for food since there's not enough space for them to grow to the point of maturity. If you decide to raise fish for eating or a local species ensure that you have adequate temperatures for the water and food.

A garden on a desktop can provide for all kinds from house plants like including lettuce as well as spinach and other herbs. Ideally, you should begin your plants with seeds in the form of a grow cube (also known as jiffy cubes) or loosely on the growth medium within your garden bed. Small seeds can be sown by placing them in between two paper towels which are kept moist and warm. Plants can also be transplanted from an existing hydroponic setup with great results.

If you are planning to transplant your garden from the soil, thoroughly clean away the dirt around the roots. Then, rinse the leaves to get rid of any pests.

The best chance of success is to have satisfaction with leafy vegetables such as spinach, lettuce and other houseplants, like anthodium, dieffenbachia, dracaena and philodendron.

You can also grow aquatic plants in your aquarium for fish. They can provide a more natural habitat for fish and help in the purification of the water.

Nitrification Cycle

Fish excreta ammonia through their wastes as well as through their gills. Ammonia in large quantities is poisonous to fish and plants. Nitrifying bacteria, which live naturally within the earth, in water and in air, first convert ammonia into nitrite before converting it to Nitrate. In an aquaponic system, the nitrifying bacteria flourish within the gravel that is used in aquarium and the growing medium of your grow beds. Nitrate is utilized by plants to flourish and grow. The plants easily absorb the nitrate present in the water, and, by consuming it, maintain the levels that are safe for fish.

System Maintenance

The only input that is daily in this system is the food of fish. For any aquarium, regular smaller feedings are superior to smaller feedings. If you do not have a massive tank, a little of food is enough. It is not recommended to feed more than your fish will eat within five minutes. The majority of tropical fish will be content with dry flake fish food, but occasionally changing their diets with brine shrimp or bloodworms can keep them in good health and more content.

The level of water within the tank will gradually diminish as some of the water is absorbed by plants while others evaporate. Every few days , replenish the tank to its highest level. Each month about 10 to 15% tank's water should be taken off and then replaced water that is fresh.

Experiment with Ideas

An aquaponic system can be an excellent instrument for experimentation and testing the validity of a theory. Below the four main theories as well as four experiments which can be conducted to test each.

Theory 1

While an aquaponics system can result in good plant growth but the hydroponic system that has precise measurements of nutrients can result in more quickly growing, better quality plants.

Experiment 1

Install a hydroponic system along with an aquaponic one. Document and monitor which is the most effective for promoting the growth of your plants.

Theory 2

An aquaponic system that is healthy has abundant nutrients to aid in the growth of leafy crops, however the plants that produce fruit will not have enough of certain elements.

Experiment 2

Plant a leafy plant like lettuce, and fruiting crops like tomatoes. Monitor to determine which one is most successful in aquaponics.

Theory 3

An acidity of 7.0 is the ideal for aquaponic systems. If the pH is lower, the nitrification process slows and the quality of water is reduced, putting stress on the fish. At an elevated pH, the plants are stressed.

Experiment 3

Set up three aquaponic system. Each one is run at various pH levels, one at 6.0 while the other is 7.0 and the last one at 8.0. Keep track of the plant's growth and health of fish at different pH levels.

Theory 4

Fish populations that are larger will encourage an increase in plant growth because of the increased amount of waste from fish and the food sources in water.

Experiment 4

Set up two aquaponic plants Stock both with one" of fish per gallon and the second with half" of fish/gallon. Examine the differences in the growth of your plants.

Chapter 4: Aquaponic Systems

Of course, there isn't only one kind of aquaponics equipment, there are a variety of options to pick from. That is among the best aspects of aquaponics. You can choose the system that will work best for your needs.

The first system I'd like to talk about is the media-filled grow beds. Grow beds that are filled with media are the most efficient aquaponics method to use. The system makes use of an aquaponics medium that is filled into tanks.

In the media-filled growth beds, the water is pumped out of the fish tanks onto the media and plants thrive within the media. The media helps ensure that the plants have sufficient nutrients and water and clean the water for fish.

There are two ways to setup this system. You could choose to utilize an 'emergency drain' system, or to build a system where the water continuously flows across the media.

The beds you will have for your plants will be approximately 12 inches in depth using this method as research has proven that this is the ideal conditions for plants to flourish in.

If you are using a flood and drain system, the water will be pumped into the growing bed of the tank, where the fish are kept. When a certain level has been reached and the water has reached that level, it will be returned to the tank along with the fish.

If you have a continuous flow system , the water will continue to flow through the roots of the plants and will continue to drain into the main tank alongside the fish. It ensures that your plants get adequate amount of nutrition along with oxygen and water as well as clean the water by allowing the bacterium in the media to convert the ammonia emitted by the waste of fish into nitrates that will ultimately be utilized by plants.

The process repeats itself repeatedly giving the plant the nutrients they require to be able to thrive without adding pesticides, insecticides , or fertilisers to plants.

The second technique is known as the nutrient-film technique. It is a hydroponic technique that is used extensively in aquaponics. If you are using the nutrient-film method, water rich in nutrients is pumped through gutters that flow over the roots continuously.

To make sure that the roots don't decay, the water flowing through the gutters is an extremely thin layer. The plants sit in small pots which are elevated above the gutter, ensuring that their roots can be allowed to access the rich nutrient water. This ensures that they can absorb the nutrients that plants require and the oxygen that the plant also requires.

The technique of nutrient film works well for small plants however when applied to larger plants, many discover it difficult to get the roots system big and the gutters get clogged up. When gutters get blocked, water is unable to traverse the gutters and instead gets stuck within the system. If the water gets stuck this causes root rot, and plants die.

If you're planning to apply the nutrient films method, be sure to apply it to tiny plants, greens, and herbs to ensure the best success in cultivating your garden.

The nutrient film method is commonly employed in commercial systems, but it is also a viable option for an aquaponics system for personal use. If you're planning to use this system at home , you must ensure your water has been cleaned prior to it being sent into the system of root since in the event that it isn't filtered, the tiny particles will adhere to the roots, causing them to be unable for the nutrients they require.

This doesn't happen in the flood and drain system since the media removes particles from the water before it gets to its root systems. It's a highly effective method, but you must be cautious when using it in your home , or your plants could be killed.

The third system is referred to by the name of deep-water culture. The plants are floats over the water. When you place the plants over the water, the roots can hang over the water, absorbing the nutrients present within the water.

While this is typically used in commercial settings it can be accomplished within your aquaponics system, and there are a variety of methods of floating your plants.

One can take on deep-water culture by making sure that the plants are floating in a raft of foam set on the fish tank's top. A common practice is cultivating fish in tanks and pumping the water through filters through long channels. The plants that are in the channels are set on floating rafts. This works similar to the technique of nutrient film in that the water flows through the channels , allowing the roots to take in the nutrients they require.

Similar to the nutrient films technique it is essential that the water be cleansed before it can be transported through the channels or the tiny particles adhere to the roots, which will cause them to be unable to take up the nutrients they require to thrive. This technique is among the most popular methods employed in commercial settings. similar to the nutrient film method, it is perfect for growing leavesy greens as well as herbs, but it doesn't work as well for plants that have larger root systems.

It is evident that, grow beds that are filled with media are the most commonly used kind of aquaponics system which is utilized to grow plants in your home. The nutrient film method as well as the deep water cultivation are both excellent systems, however they are typically used in commercial settings , and don't allow you to plant plants with larger root systems.

Chapter 5: Best Aquaponic Plants

As with fish, you can cultivate a range of aquatic plants due to the garden's energy-efficient and cost-effective attributes, it'll make it easier to grow healthy plants with minimal effort.

The most beneficial plants you can plant in your aquaponic garden are ones that grow over the soil and have roots that require constantly moist. These are some great examples that will get you started.

1. Tomatoes

If you are planning to grow tomatoes, you require an adequate aquarium. The staple of salad requires plenty of nutrients to flourish because it goes through different transformations. There are two kinds of tomatoes. The first one is known as determinate. This plant type produces fruits all year long. In contrast the indeterminate varieties will only produce fruit for a certain month and time. The good part about tomatoes that are indeterminate is that their fruits will be more durable than determinate varieties.

If you're an aquaponic grower, you should select the determinate tomatoes as their compact frame is suitable for aquariums for fish. It's also a great plant for newbies as it is easy to determine the precise timing for harvesting the fruits.

To be able to grow the plants, it is necessary to set them up in a humid area. They also require separate seeds tray. Be sure to provide them with at minimum eight hours of sunshine, especially during the fruiting stage.

2. Lettuce

Lettuce is one the most easy plants to grow inside an aquaponic planter. It is possible to plant iceberg lettuce, or more leafy counterparts. The plant is thriving if the temperature of the air is 75 degrees F. The roots are, however require warm water with temperatures of 70 degrees Fahrenheit. This is why lettuce is an ideal companion to tilapia.

The lettuce seedlings into the growing bed, or you can put them in a small tray for seedlings. After that, you can start transplanting the lettuce plants as when they began to sprout. When collecting these plants it is advised that you don't pull the roots, but only just a handful of leaves at each time. This is so that they are productive throughout the year.

3. Cabbages

Like cabbage, they are thought of as a main ingredient in many cuisines in China. Its seeds need at least one week for germinating. Additionally, cabbages require at least 45 days to grow. Be sure that your plants are placed in a humid environment with temperatures of 70 degrees Fahrenheit, so that it will grow in a healthy way. As soon as the cabbages begin to grow, you can transfer them to the grow beds.

4. Melons and Cucumbers

The two plants are classified as vines and each of them has similar requirements. You can build an trellis to help them grow or put them in the upper parts of the growing bed.

In general, the cucumbers and melons thrive in places where it is at least 75% humidity every day. It can take at least 2 months for these plants to grow to maturity. They are at their peak of productivity in the first 12 weeks. But, they will continue producing plenty of fruits over the months.

Chapter 6: Plants

4.1 PLANT BIOLOGY

What are your goals as a Grower?

Like all living things on earth, are carbon-based creatures They use carbon to reproduce, grow and even survive. The most significant carbon sugar chains utilized by plants are cellulose sucrose, fructose, and. While plants are carbon-based but they are mostly composed from water. The majority of crops that are grown in aquaponics systems and greenhouses have between 87-93 percent water. The importance of water to plants is obvious!

What is the source of water for the PLANT?

Water is the most affordable construction material for the plant. Other materials, such carbon and photosynthates require an enormous amount of energy to procure which is why plants are dependent on the more readily available materials in the greatest extent feasible.

The plants use water extensively in their structures. They make use of the less abundant element carbon to build "containers" as well as to increase the force and pressure by using water, they make the structure stronger. It is then a plant cell that is which is the element that makes up the plant. It is one of the amazing things plants can do to allow them to reproduce, grow, live, and carry out photosynthesis. (Plants are very efficient in collecting sunlight and then converting the energy into chemical energy, far more efficient than what we can achieve using our technology today!)

In general, plants utilize water for numerous purposes like:

*Growth

Removing the hydrogen in water

*Transpiration (to cool the plant or alter the environment of the plant)

*Photosynthesis

*As an solvent

As a vehicle used to transport nutrients

WATER USE VASCULAR TISSUE MOVE INSIDE THE PLANT

Phloem and the xylem are two kinds of vascular tissue in plants that move nutrients and water up and down. It also photosynthizes down.

WATER AND CARBON GO HAND-IN-HAND.

Plants can't survive without carbon and can't exist without water. Both resources are interdependent. Carbon is the primary building block, while water serves as the solvent for life. It is impossible to live without water.

4.2 ENVIRONMENTAL NEEDS OF PLANTS

While the appearance of plants is simple They're actually very sophisticated CATED MACHINES

Simply put plants are comprised of several different kinds of tissues: roots stems and leaves. The roots extend into the media, and then branch out taking nutrients, interacting with microorganisms and trading resources with the fungi holding and supporting stems and many more. Stems offer support, add the leaf height and transport water and nutrients from the roots.

Note: Plant growth. The plants don't develop from every part of the stem, or extend all at all at. Instead, they grow upwards only from the top (the apical mesistem) and then only extends outwards from the sides (lateral expansion). This growth is fueled by photosynthesis and the resources are carefully and economically distributed by the plant in order to increase its size while remaining healthy.

Note that the meristem is the growth portion of the plant. Meristematic cells are not differentiated (they aren't being altered for a particular purpose as of yet) until their use is determined by the plant hormones.

There are a myriad of kinds of tissues. They perform many functions in order to reproduce and grow. They're extremely advanced and thrilling! In our current situation we'll keep this information simple and introductory , and leave the more intricate details to the future Plant Biology course. You should however, consider the following as general guidelines; I can assure you that for each of these common rules and traits There are some plants out in the world that have exemptions.

ROOT ANCHORING, UPTAKE NUTRIENTS and HOST MICROBES

At the root the plants absorb the nitrate, phosphate, potassium and magnesium, calcium, and chloride, usually in the form of an ions in water. The nutrients are carried through the stem and into the leaves where they're taken up and converted to produce something other.

Apart from moving water and nutrients The roots also anchor the plant and serve as a link between roots, shoots, and the soil. It's crucial to understand that the soil's environment is mostly an aquatic one A film of the soil's particles provides an ecosystem which plants are able to benefit from. The soil environment functions as an energy-gathering system (almost as a general storage facility for fungi and microbes) in the ecological system.

ROOT ZONES HAVE a history of issues when There is a deficiency of OXYGEN OR IF MICROBIAL COUNTIES are involved.

In an aquaponics system the root system provides the means of capturing the nutrients and trade them. This gives the plant to access the nutrients and materials it would not be able to obtain otherwise. The most significant aspect of that economics is the microbes that are often found in the roots as a habitat. While this is usually beneficial, it could cause problems as when you remove these roots, you strip out the microbes' home (BSA*) and disrupt the system's biology and disrupting the process of nitrification.

*BSA as well as SSA (biological as well as specific area) are essential to root system of the plant. In reality the roots are able to create some quantity of area and a large proportion of reactions occur within that area.

One of the most important requirements within the root zones is the oxygen. The processes happening in the root zone consume oxygen and when roots are starved of oxygen, it opens up the path for diseases. Thus, certain media may be harmful to the health of your plant because it does not allow sufficient oxygen to the roots.

PLANT STEMS ARE RIGID SUPPORTS THAT hold up, are ORIENT, AND AT-TACH THE LEAVES TO ROOT SYSTEM(TEM).

When we speak of plants, it is necessary to be talking about plants within the context of a group. The planet is designed to encourage communities. Every organism can exist on its own.

Every aspect of a stem develops as a result of different organisms and other elements. The stem changes the direction the plant is facing to ensure that it can receive more sunlight when in the face of competition (a relationship) to other organisms , or as a response to environmental factors. It gives support to leaves so that they can withstand the elements like trampling, wind, and other environmental factors. It also provides "plumbing" through the roots through the stem up to the foliage (again this all within all the framework of being part of an ecosystem).

The LEAVES ARE THE ENERGY PRODUCTION and GAS EXCHANGE CENTERS of the PLANT

The plant's leaves are the main energy sources for the plants. They are where all the chemical processes are performed however, they are also susceptible to being damaged. Leaves are among the first things plants develop following the time of germination. They begin as embryonic leaf (very the first leaves, also known as plumule) and are soon followed by mature (true) leaves. True leaves are the ones that produce energy for the plant. Most of the photosynthesis takes place in leaves that are designed to absorb sunlight and use sunlight. A lot of plants move and twist to catch the greatest amount of sunlight. (This is known as phototropism.)

Leaves are also the place where most gas exchange takes place. Carbon dioxide enters while photosynthetic reactions happen and $H_2O + O_2$ go out.

The leaves are often in fact the primary product we use that we as gardeners. Because the plant uses leaves, growers usually follow this "one-third" rule and should never take more than one third of the plant. So plants have these energy centers to power the stem, root, and leaf growth, all of which are very demanding processes. Any more removal can lead to stress on the plant, which often causes disease and die-back issues.

4.3 SPLITS in the AQUAPONIC SYSTEM
PEST CONTROL

The fish that live in your aquaponic system can limit the way you control pests. If you are in hydroponics and employ soaps, oils copper products or pyrethrin to control pests In aquaponics, the using these products could be detrimental to the health of your fish.

The best way to do this is to choose the best plants, the correct fish, and use the appropriate method. Plants which are more resistant to insects (e.g. Elenora Basil is resistant to downy mildew, which can help to avoid the use of copper sulfur.).

Choose fish that are hardy. A good example is common carp that are hardy and can withstand almost everything. Contrary to that, a fish like trout is more sensitive. If you're anticipating disease-related issues and expect to manage the problem with a treatment which could impact your fish, it is important to select a fish that is able to handle the issue.

The best method to use will determine the type and method of controls you are able to apply. In ZipGrow Towers such as the tower housing shields the soil and stops pesticides from entering the water. This , in comparison to media bed or a trough is a major advantage.

The final solution is to implement a successful IPM strategy.

System design also gives the user more control of the system. We're hugely in favor of separate systems. Fish are kept in one area while our plant life in a different and there's a door between the two spaces that we can close to keep the two sides separate. This isn't just for economic reasons (space for plants to grow is costly, space for growing fish isn't) but also allows the possibility of doing things like fog without the need for contact with fish.

ENVIRONMENTAL

The interesting thing about aquaponics is that the systems cannot be designed to support plants. they have to be compromised in order in order for plants to support the other elements that make up the whole system. It is important to take into consideration the impact of this compromise, as plants are the most important output in the entire system. The majority of your energy and time are devoted to the growth of plants.

The environmental factors such as CO_2, humidity, temperature and light may be significant variables that can

control because you have to manage because you must match it to the fish and plants.

If you're growing wasabi for instance, you'll be capable of keeping something similar to trout. Both prefer cooler temperatures. In contrast watercress thrives in an environment that is warm and swampy;

it will help to increase it within the same system like it is tilapia. This is yet another instance where the separation of your system can be beneficial to you.

The key point is that you should develop within a larger ecological framework. Each individual is individual, and while I will give you the basics but the method you use to discover your system will depend on your particular system.

NUTRIENT DEFICIENCY

Deficiencies are more prevalent when aquaponics systems are used. In contrast, hydroponic farmers have more specific requirements, better-formulated management abilities and grow more limited varieties of crops Aquaponic growers are risk-takers. There is no clear outcomes. The composition of your feed is different from month-to-month. There are more inputs.

A solution is to test tissues and water to detect deficiency and to respond appropriately. It is always necessary to be thinking creatively and actively solving any issues you spot.

Although some things are more difficult to do with aquaponics systems I'll assure you that the highest yields I've seen are from aquaponic systems.

4.4 UTILES FOR PLANTS

The goal of this focus is to assist you to understand your market more precisely.

There are five main applications for aquaponics. They are not the identical to your markets however, each market typically only serves one purpose and the reason you're there can help you choose the most profitable market (or in reverse).

HOBBY

If you're growing your business as an interest you're selling your products to the marketplace of yourself or your family members, your neighbors or your close friends, etc. Perhaps you're using aquaponics as it gives you the satisfaction of creating something that is unique. Perhaps you choose to do it because you believe that you can produce better food than a farmer. You might do it because there isn't a single store selling watercress near you and it's a favorite food item.

COMMERCIAL

It is essential in order to determine the "why" for this application as Opex (operating expense) as well as Capex (capital expenses) are usually more expensive for aquaponics. The only method to answer this question for commercial use is to put it in an a dollar symbol. In this case, for instance, you may utilize aquaponics to grow commercially as you'll earn more profit from the organic produce of aquaponics.

Marketing

A lot farmers in our area are cultivating simultaneously aquaponically and hydroponically. They run both systems simultaneously. The reason they do this is because aquaponics is fun and fascinating. It's a stunning combination of value and ecology as well as having a tremendous advertising value. It provides context for the things they're doing. It sparks conversations. It attracts people as well as makes the farm seem exotic.

Community

If you're trying to grow an entire community by using aquaponics, then you're doing so to help build communities. It can also be used to support marketing too.

EDUCATION

Education is often closely linked to the community. Aquaponic systems can be amazing tools for learning. They can be used to teach agriculture, ecology and engineering, chemistry, and many more in a fascinating method.

The bottom line is to think carefully about your market.

Chapter 7: Fish, Plants And Bacteria

As previously mentioned the three main players in an aquaponics system each having its own function to perform. This chapter will assist you to get a better knowledge of each and every one of them, so keep reading!

Fish

Fish are essential in an aquaponics. They supply the plants with nutrients and are an important source of protein for your family. It is crucial to choose the correct fish species that will thrive in an aquaponics setup. Also, select a native species that is able to adapt well to the local climate and the natural climate. Tilapia is recommended living in tropical areas, and in cooler regions trout is the ideal most suitable choice. Also, select a species that is able to live and reproduce in tanks. Find fish breed fingerlings readily available in your neighborhood. Also, look for breeds that do not feed on one another.

Diverse types varieties of fish could be raised in aquaponics systems. When choosing which kind of fish to grow it is crucial to know what you are looking for to get out of your system. Do you want to raise fish as an alternative to food or as an ornament?

A few of the kinds of edible fish that are typically raised in an aquaponics system include trout, carp, tilapia jade perch perch, catfish cod, barramundi and cod. The ornamental fish that are raised are typically goldfish and koi. Other aquatic creatures can be kept in the aquarium, such as crayfish mussels and Prawns.

In feeding your fish ensure that you choose a food source that is suitable for their protein needs. Slugs, plant bugs, caterpillars, and insect larvae in plants are a fantastic alternative to fish for food. While you are providing the fish with food, but you also protect your plants from harm.

How many fish you should include in your tank? This is dependent upon the dimensions of your aquarium and the kind of system that is used. It is also important to consider the volume of plants to consider. There must be enough plants that can filter the water. For those who are new to fishing, it is best to start small by selecting low density. There's a rule or rule of thumb that one kilogram of a fully grown fish should be able to hold 8 to 10 gallons water. The ratio for fingerlings is 1/10 of a pound for every 8 to 10 gallons water.

Plants

It is possible to plant everything, including trees! However, different plants thrive in different locations. Select plants that thrive locally in your region and according to the time of year. The trick is to cultivate perennial plants in a group. In the winter and fall seasons you can plant cold-season plants. During warmer seasons, plant tropical plants.

Be sure that your plants receive the correct amount of light, water pH along with temperature and the space. The pH of water in aquaponics is between 6.8 to 7.0 Certain plants do not work in an aquaponics. Blueberries and raspberries thrive in soils that are acidic, with pH less than 6.8. However, Zinnias calendula and chrysanthemums thrive in soils that are alkaline and pH greater than 7.

Examples of plants being grown in aquaponics are lettuce and bok choi. Kale and arugula, swiss chard and mint. watercress, chives and coriander, parsley, thyme and sage. watercress and rosemary. Certain plants can thrive when tanks of fish are full of fish. They require more nutrients. This includes tomatoes peppers, cucumbers, chili, beans, peas, beans and cucumbers. They also include strawberry beans, peas, broccoli, squash and cabbage. There are also those who have tried growing bananas and dwarf trees , such as citrus, lemon and peach.

Growing plants for aquaponics can be done in a variety of ways to grow. It is possible to scatter small seeds all over the surface of the bed. This works for lettuce and carrots. The method of germinating in damp towels is suitable for larger seeds which germinate quickly, such as beans and peas. If you wish to stay clear of the stress beginning seeds you can purchase seedslings-a small plant. Prior to placing the seedlings in the garden bed, you should shake the soil off the roots and then put it under water to get rid of any remaining soil. It is suggested to place the seaweed extract or worm juice into a container of water and then gently swish them to eliminate the soil. The extracts of seaweed and worm juice will help the seedlings to establish themselves in a new location and avoid shock from transplantation.

Aquaponics allows us to place plants two times closer one another than in soil farming, because all the nutrients as well as oxygen and water that are required by plants are at the level of the roots. Therefore, the roots don't have to be stretched out as deep. However, it is important to consider the size of the plant when spacing out to allow the airflow between plants, let in light and to avoid bugs and fungus.

Fish and plants live in one place, therefore the density of the plants is correlated to the size of the fish. It is one square foot or 0.1 square meter for 1 pounds of fish. Start adding plants at the beginning of the cycle.

Bacteria

Nitrifying bacteria are one of the most powerful elements that act as a link between fish and plants. In the past, bacteria convert the waste of fish into fertilizers for plants. In the absence of this connection, the process won't work.

There are two distinct bacteria that perform this crucial role: Nitrosomonas along with Nitrobacter. There are usually bad bacteria present in the system. Nitrifying bacteria don't just process waste from fish and toxins, but also combat bad bacteria that reside in the the intestines of fish and on plant roots, and also prevent them from resurfacing.

Chapter 8: The Parts That Make Up The

Balance Parts

Once you've got a an understanding of the general principles and the main components of your aquaponic system it's time to learn certain aspects. The effectiveness of your system depends on the balance you can achieve within your system. So, it's crucial to find the correct balance of organisms that will make your system run efficiently.

This chapter will cover important information you should be aware of the major components of your aquaponics system. It is also important to establish the right equilibrium between these components.

Finding the ideal balance

Any disturbance in your system could cause issues that could hinder growth or even endanger the most vulnerable part of your eco-system: your fish.

The presence of too few bacteria colonies within your system mean that ammonia won't be effectively treated. This could lead to accumulation of ammonia within the aquarium, and ultimately it could cause death of the fish.

If there is a shortage of plant species, the levels of nitrates as well as Nitrites in the water will build up. However, they don't always cause harm to fish, their high concentration can affect the ecosystem, including the pH levels and the oxygen levels within the waters.

A fish population that is too small is a sign that there is not enough ammonia bacteria to transform. This could result in a lack of nutrients to support optimal growth of plants.

The ratios

Since that the equilibrium of your aquaponic setup can be so crucial, there are certain systems ratios that are in the system. The ratio can be determined by calculating the input and the output you wish to attain. It is going to be calculated the number of plants you would like to build as well as the final output and how many fish are required and how much food they will need to consume to produce enough nutrition for these plants, or as an input.

In order to get the output

This output from your machine is determined by calculating the area you can use to grow your product. Of course, this will depend on the type of food you're planning to grow in addition to the degree of nutrition and the amount of space they require.

On a larger commercial scale, production is usually determined by the number of plants and the length of time required for the harvest to take place. However, calculating the amount of space needed to grow your own produce even if you're cultivating them for your own use ought to be easy and straightforward.

Input

The amount of input your aquaponic system requires is contingent on the specific requirements of the plants grow in your backyard. You'll be calculating how much fish feed is required to provide the required nutrients. Here's a general outline for daily inputs. Note that leafy greens require less input than fruits.

.2 pounds of nutrients per sq meter or about 45g per square inch leafy greens

.3 pounds of nutrition per square foot, or 60 to 80 grams for each square inch fruit plants

If you're planning to plant a small amount of each, estimate each according to your needs and calculate the minimum daily requirements.

The fish factor

After you've determined the amount of input you require and then you'll be able to determine the amount of fish you'll will need to feed. The numbers of fish are calculated in terms of biomass, which is the weight of your whole fish population, not the individual numbers.

Fishes at different stages of development consume their food in different ways. Fingerlings consume 10 percent of their weight in fish food while juveniles and adults consume 2 percent of their body weight during the course of a day. Then you can divide the amount of input you require in by .1 (for fingerslings) as well as .02 (for juveniles and adults).

When you've got the biomass, it's time to estimate the number of fish you'll require. Fingerlings average fifty grams, or 1.7 an ounce as adults and juveniles weigh between 60-500 grams or 2-18 pounds according to the species. All you need be able to do is multiply the amount of biomass you require by the weight average of the fish, and you're set.

The density of the fish tank

This is the amount of fish that you can keep in the tank. The density of your tanks must not exceed 44 pounds per 16 gallons or 20 kgs per 1000 liters. Anything more than that could make fish sick and alter their feeding habits and create the need for additional air pumps.

Bio-filters

The bio-filters are where you can find your bacteria's friends, therefore shouldn't be overly large as this may cause them to be susceptible to lower temperatures, as well as fluctuating ammonia levels and pH levels.

Bio-filters are typically filled with porous media that have greater surface area for the bacteria to grow. As a general rule is that you'll require 3.5 gallon of bio-filter or seven gallons of the growing media to hold enough bacterial growth for processing one ounce of fish feed daily. This is why you'll need 500ml of biofilter to make 1 gram feed each day.

Be aware you have other factors which could impact the balance of your organisms and nutrients in your body. That means you shouldn't completely rely on ratio guidelines. In the end it's an experiment and you'll be able to gain more knowledge about the condition of your system by conducting regular tests. Change the ratios as necessary and be sure to record the changes you observe.

Chapter 9: Utilizing Media Beds

I would encourage you to go through this chapter to find out the main reasons Aquaponics experts recommend home media beds as a hobby. Media beds offer many benefits for those who want to become aquaponic gardeners. Commercial aquaponic farms are adding media beds more into their systems.

Using Media Bed Benefits

Media Beds are beds for growing which are filled with some kind of gravel or rock. Media is a fancy name for any item that is used in a garden without soil environment to help support plants. Perlite, rock, sand or styrofoam clay beads, and mineral fiber are just a few examples of these media. (Since the majority of aquaponic gardeners utilize the expanded form of shale, gravel, or clay beads, we'll employ the term rocks to refer to the media in the remainder part of this book.) Media beds are usually heavier than beds for growing which only contain water as even the lightest of rocks weigh more than water.

But the advantages that the media bed offers are worth it. With centuries of knowledge, you'll be capable of filling your bed in a comfortable way with the materials suggested. Learn how to effectively establish the process of flow and ebb that ensures that your roots are supplied with oxygen and water.

DEFINITION

Media beds are grow bed that is lined with an neutral or inert material to help support the plants that are growing within the beds. The most used aquaponics media are clay pellets that have been expanded and spread shale. The ideal is for these materials to be greater than 3/4 inches in size in order to allow adequate drainage feasible.

Plant Varieties

The addition of media provides something to keep your plants' attention. It is possible to grow tiny plants, roots and even trees as you're making use of media. I wouldn't recommend beginning your aquaponic journey by trying to establish a papaya plant or a the banana-tree grove.

However, filling your growing beds with gravel can give you the opportunity to explore a larger range of plants than water by itself could produce.

You can plant massive, tall plants such as this banana tree by making use of media in your beds.

There is no way to grow anything in a bed of media. Aquaponics' only restriction is to cultivate plants that thrive in the pH range suitable for your species of fish (6.0 up to 7.0).

Mineralization

Mineralization is the process of reduction or oxidation in organic substances, to make them available to plants. Your media surfaces are huge areas that are constantly bathed by the fish tank with oxygenated water as well as organic waste. This is the ideal conditions for turning the fish waste to plant-based nutrients. When you need to remove the waste of fish from the environment, you're removing the nutrients you originally added in the form of diet of fish into the environment. The process of allowing the media to transform the waste into nutrients naturally will boost the amount of vitamins in your plants. It will also help you to plant plants that are polluted to benefit from using water as a method.

Protection of roots from light and Solids

The light can harm the roots and hinder them from taking in the nutrients and water that your plants require. The delicate hairs roots make use of for storing water have been destroyed by oil. Algae can develop on surfaces that are exposed to light, and some roots may be green when trying to photosynthesis. In a media-filled area, the plant's roots lie beneath the layer of media which prevents burning. Algae are found in the surfaces of moist surfaces and media, however the surface algae is not as the blooms of algae that grow in tanks that are filled with water. The water that comes out of your tank of fish is awash of tiny particles that are organic. What remains of the soil settles down on roots of a rising bed, which is simply filled with water, blocking their capacity to absorb nutrients and water.

However rising beds, systems with no media utilize a number of filters to remove the particles. In a media bed certain fish waste particles build up on the surface of your media sheet, making sure that your plant's roots are well-nourished, thus reducing the need for further filters in the majority of instances.

SOUNDS FISHY

I would suggest using pea gravel, sand or other tiny particles in place of clay pellets or rocks. Fish solids are known to block the gravel with sand or pea, which prevents oxygen from getting into the roots. For novice gardeners experienced aquaponic gardeners recommend that the media be at least 3/4 inches (19 millimetres) in the thickness.

Flood and Drain

The Grow Bed advantages of media beds is the ability to remove the water and leave the plants in a dry, high-pressure environment. It is not a good idea to keep the beds dry however, for your plants you'll want to provide oxygen and air into the root zone. Plant roots get regular access to oxygen and water by permitting the media beds to fill up and drain after every hour. This oxygen encourages quick strong growth of your plants.

Worms

Worms is a greenhouse's gold. They consume decaying matter, and transform it into worm castings making great fertilizer. A bed that is rising with media provides plenty of room for worms and provides the ideal natural fertilizer right in the middle of in the area where your plants can absorb the nutrients. You might be wondering how creatures will survive when the bed is constantly inundated. Worms absorb oxygen through their skins and water will not kill worms as us. Worms die only when oxygen is present. They are happy to be in water even if the atmosphere is filled with oxygen.

Great for Landscaping

We usually think about growing crops with aquaponics. There's no reason why you shouldn't utilize aquaponics to improve the landscape of your property. Through the combination of a fish pond with plants and trees planted in decorative beds, media farming can help the plants grow without costly irrigation systems. It is best if you live in a climate which doesn't freeze or when a structure of any type helps protect the natural landscape.

Utilize Media Beds have drawbacks

Certain things are good. There are some drawbacks of putting media in your beds for growing These media typically add weight to the bed as compared to just growing in water. the media can become blocked and alter the water's chemistry.

Helping to support a Grow Bed with Rocks

The aquaponic bed that is with water in it requires substantial support from the ground up. The introduction of more heavy media other than water will make the weight increase by the 62 pounds per cubic foot to up to 100 pounds. However, a small device could easily fit in any enough space to accommodate the weight of a person. A bed that is filled by wet dirt weighs 3350 pounds when it is at 12 inches of depth. Add on the weight of the rising bed and the water itself and an elevated bed of up to 4,000 pounds or 2 tons could be as large as the bed. It's about the size of the size of a pickup truck, which is it's a safe place to park the truck that you can put the garden. The best place to put it is a level backyard. dirt can support up to 200 pounds of weight per square foot. Concrete slab foundations typically support at least 100 pounds of weight per square foot considering that they may be the foundation that supports the lowest floor of your home. Within the United States the average ranking for a floor that is residential has been 40lbs per sq ft. Utilizing stacking cinderblocks is one the least expensive ways to assist garden grow. They aren't a threat to termites which is why it's unlikely they'll be a problem for lumber that's higher than 18 inches above the ground. Turn a few stacks of blocks with two boards and you'll be able to support the majority of beds that are rising. If you are supporting a long grow bed using wooden legs or cinderblocks placing supports every 3-4 feet is recommended. If you're concerned about the movement of these blocks, with concrete surface bonds, you could join the stacks. In addition to preventing the blocks from moving to one another, this can provide your support columns with an appealing, smooth look. It is possible to support your via beds, in addition to having a wooden structure on four legs. The main issue with wood legs is that they pose the chance of being damaged to the wooden legs from water or insects when they come in contact with ground. However, if the idea of a wooden stand seems appealing, sealing of the legs' ends the legs using epoxy can help reduce water and insect damage.

Then, you'll have the option to buy shelves or metal stands designed to hold thousands of pounds. For hobbyists at home Many hardware stores carry high-end shelving shelves that are typically able to accommodate the weight of 300 pounds of weight per shelf. From my own experience, I've learned that Rubbermaid oval tanks (50and 100 gallon capacities) are able to fit into the support of a 2' sturdy shelf. In the end, commercial shelving options exist that will give more than enough capacity for load-bearing.

Green TIP

There are a variety of ways to raise your bed's height to waist height can help. A raised bed is less difficult to deal with, drains more effectively, and is elevated above ground , which helps prevent the damage caused by termites, which is essential when you build the growing bed of wood.

System Clogging

Grow bed filters may clog in time, regardless of whether you use 3/4-inch rocks. If the beds become clogged and oxygen is not able to reach the roots in the soil. Without oxygen, roots begin decaying, rotting and smelly. The root balls that are thick are the most frequent cause of clogging within media beds. This is because the roots are unable to supply their oxygen supply. There are two indicators which indicate that there is a problem through the bed prior to you start to recognize an issue. The first is a sudden increase in pH, which indicates that a area of the bed may not receive enough oxygen anymore. In Chapter 10, we'll discuss how to determine your pH. In the second, you may notice an insufficient amount of flow that could traverse the room that you can't solve by flushing the drain.

PH Specifications of Your Media

pH is the measurement of whether water is neutral, acidic or alkaline. Media also influence the level of pH in your body. Your media could affect two ways on the chemistry in your body. I've mentioned before that the pH level of the bed will increase dramatically if some of the bed is blocked. This is often caused by a large mature plant as roots are able to bind themselves so tightly to the medium that oxygen and water can not penetrate the middle inside the ball. Tomato plants that have been growing for more than nine months are known for their huge, thick root balls like this. Luckily, the pH fluctuations that are associated with root balls can be easily corrected by removing the plants that are most likely to be the cause of the problem. In the event that you accidentally remove something that did not cause damage, it could be quickly replanted in the majority of media beds. It should not be pH neutral for the media in itself. This is usually done by using river rocks or stone rocks. Soft minerals, like marble and calcareous dissolve in water, and help keep the pH high. If you purchase your rock from a salesperson, they will be able to verify they are neutral pH. However, even although the rocks themselves are pH neutral but they need to have a coating of sand, or other particles which will help maintain the pH. I recommend that you wash the rocks with a bath of water before placing them in your growing bed. You can reuse multiple piles of rock using the same tub of water. The washing of these rocks can decrease the quantity of silt as well as sand which is absorbed into your garden and prevents the formation of a clog in your bed.

Media Options

Your choice of media is vital. If you've selected the right type of rock, it's likely that you'll keep those rocks for years to in the future. The weight and cost of your options vary greatly. You could ask a third party to complete the task, and then take delivery of specially designed, lightweight media to aquaponics. Or, you can purchase inexpensive but and sharp rocks to help keep costs low.

* Gravel
* River rock
* Clay pellets expanded
* Expanded Shale
* Volcanic gravel is also the least costly option, costing as little in price as $0.20 per gallon as well as $1.50 for each cubic foot. It is easily available and is a good option. For instance, it could be impressive to have an ever-growing bed of granite chips. Unfortunately, the most heavy option is probably wet gravel at about 105 pounds per cubic foot.

It also has sharp edges that can cut flesh. The heavy weight as well as sharp edge make it extremely difficult to deal with, which means you aren't moving your plants around as you would with clay pellets expanded in lighter medium. Hardware stores in your area are an excellent source of gravel, but you'll only spend dollars on a large amount of items if you locate a retailer that specializes in stones and rocks. It is possible to purchase rocks in bulk, and then transport huge bags of gravel to your home. Even if the gravel appears "clean" to sell but you might want to clean it yourself.

River Rock

The stone is called river rock, with the edges shattered due to tumbling in rivers, streams or oceans over many years. It is the same hardness as dirt when wet, with 100 pounds per cubic foot. Its weight makes it tough to work with, and the smooth edges won't scratch the skin. However, the price is low for the river rock ($1.50 per cubic foot) and the smooth edges make it an appealing alternative. My first wide-bodied device was made using river rocks. I filled a 50-gallon tank onto my van's backand drove to the rock shopand began and then sifted river rocks into the tank. Then, after the store assessed my vehicle's weight, they I was paid in the amount of the different. I've been charged less than $11 for the 50 gallons of rock. I'm prepared to pay a higher price for something less complicated and more work-friendly after enduring it for a couple of months. However, large rocks in a field in which you plan to plant trees or grow high-growing crops, could aid in the process.

Expanded Clay Pellets

The light-weight clay pellets created specifically for hydroponics. The clay balls that are rounded weigh so little that even when dry, they remain floating in the water. They weigh only 75 pounds for each cubic foot when they are wet. The term Hydroton which is a type that is expanded clay pellets created in Germany are common. In summer 2012 however it was announced that the Hydroton line of clay pellets withdrawn. Because these clay pellets are small they are typically only see them in hydroponic catering stores. The 50-liter bags cost around $60 when I built my backyard system. This is $35 per cubic foot, compared to $1.50 per cubic feet I spent on the rocks in the shore.

Prices for larger clay pellets vary based on the location you reside in. I was able to find clay pellets for 50-liter bags in Florida during 2011 at less than $30. Still expensive, but not as expensive as the ones I was originally charging.

Green TIP

If you're not buying at a nearby hydroponics retailer be aware of cost of shipping. While clay balls aren't as expensive as they are in retail stores but getting them delivered to your doorstep could be more expensive. With the growing popularity of aquaponics and more popular, you may be able to purchase clay balls that are specifically designed for aquaponics from big box retailers like Lowe's, Home Depot, and Walmart to pick up locally. The pressure never hurts!

Expanded shale is a light material found in early 1900's. In a revolving kiln slate or shale are baked, which causes it to expand similar to popcorn kernels heated in the oven are able to do. Extended shale brands and extended slates comprise Haydite Stalite, Haydite, as well as Utalite. The shale that is expanded looks like gravel, however the method of production seems to smooth off sharp edges. The shale that is expanded isn't the same weight as expanded clay balls, but it weighs only 85 pounds for each cubic feet, and that's not bad at all. Since the beginning, expanded shale has been used extensively in the construction industry to create concrete structures that are lightweight and improve drainage in the landscape. It's available at a fraction of the cost if you're lucky enough to be near an aggregate company which has expanded shale available for sale. In 2011 my mother was capable of loading 250 tons of expanded shale into her truck at an adjacent quarry. It cost approximately $1.50 in cubic feet. The hydroponics industry has launched extended marketing of shale. The brand's name can be Rocks. The reason for this is that the expanded shale is produced from the U.S. which appeals to people who are concerned about the environment and ensuring that the carbon footprint of their products is reduced. The expanded shale that is sold to niche aquaponics and hydroponics markets has been carefully analyzed in order to determine its stability the pH ranges. The prices are comparable for expanded clay pellets expanded shale offered to gardeners. Another option is to have your local aquaponic enthusiasts ' network examined. There are people who will allow whom you can place the bulk purchase, thus reducing the cost.

As the dissolved gases expand as magma is cooled the scoria from volcanic rock (also known as cinders) develops. Scoria typically grows upon volcanic flux surface. If dry, Scoria only barely falls into the water, and is surrounded by tiny fissures. This makes it ideal for aquaponic systems. Scoria weighs about 85 kilos per cubic foot. The cost of scoria, or cinders varies based on the proximity to a source of volcanic activity the area you live in. Scoria is extremely affordable in Hawaii and is known due to its volcanic eruptions.

The most important thing you need to Be able to

* Media Betting is growing rock-filled beds or another inert medium to support the plants.

* Growing beds that are based on media can significantly enhance the variety of plants you are able to be able to successfully cultivate because nutrients minerize themselves in the growing beds.

* Beds with media would be difficult unless they have small stones. Be sure that your garden is properly placed and is therefore secured.

* Don't use media or sand with smaller that 3/4 inch. Sort out smaller rocks and sand, which could cause obstruction to your system.

* Both river and gravel rocks are easily purchased. If you're looking for lighter rocks, or someone else to wash the rocks, anticipate paying for it.

Chapter 10: What Can Grow Through The

Aquaponic System?

5.1 How to Choose the Plants: Deciding Which to Plant and when to plant it

I have friends who've grown just about everythingfrom potatoes to trees. Aquaponics allows you to cultivate almost anything, but you must remember some things when making a decision on which plants to grow.

The first thing to remember is that you should plant plants that you can consume. I do not usually think it is logical to grow numerous kales if they don't eat them or even like they. It is also important to ensure that you have plants in your unit. Say perhaps you've constructed a basic system using one IBC with a single planter bed on top of the IBC and a fish tank. Be sure to not remove the plants at the same time since you'll be left with nothing to bring nutrients from the unit. Ideally, you'll have a wide mix of plants within this unit, at any instance: seeds, half-grown plants and mature plants at the same time. In this way, you'll be able to move through the plant life, take rid of mature plants and plant a second one to fill in the gaps. While making sure you have plenty of plants to utilize the nutrients.

Other important aspects to take into consideration

It is also important to remember that different plants grow under different conditions. Before you start growing it is important to begin by determining the kind of garden bed you'll need to choose. It is determined by the root structure that plants generally possess. Plants that don't have a structure for their roots require floating beds, while root vegetables thrive in growing in wicking gardens (aquaponics). Most other plants will grow most efficiently with media beds.

For plants like leaves, lettuce, or even herbs, it's recommended to choose floating beds that resemble a 'raft. For root vegetables, the wicking beds would be the best option. If you're looking to plant peppers, beans, tomatoes and a lot of other varieties of multi-yielding plants then the media beds may be the best choice.

Another crucial aspect to consider is choosing the ideal location you will set up your aquaponics farm. The temperature of the surrounding as well as the amount of sunlight, wind and rain are all important aspects to take into consideration to create healthy plants. If you want to grow your plants outdoors, search for varieties of vegetables that thrive in your environment. In addition, certain areas may have you use greenhouses. However, you don't need to be concerned, as you can build an indoor garden, should you wish.

Try as hard as you can to not fight Mother Nature even if you decide to install greenhouses. It's often difficult to regulate the temperature. The best plants flourish when temperatures are consistent with their normal processes. So, in winter months, try to cultivate cold-weather plants and during summer, it is necessary to plant warm-weather plants. Check out these images to find out more about:

Also, it is important plan your planting time carefully. If you wish to ensure an adequate amount of food for an extended period of time, be sure you plan your harvests so which ensures that your crops don't get ripe simultaneously. This could cause wasted product as well as the in-between times/periods during which your system isn't producing any product. If your goal is to produce multiples of a particular kind of vegetable, you can try increasing the duration of your growing by roughly the length of time it will take to eat one batch.

It's the harvest (and certain of the most delicious vegetables to begin with)

If you're trying to include more variety in the food you eat, then might consider overlapping the growth times that you can combine three varieties of vegetables. It could take quite time to master this method so that it's in line with your consumption habits as well as the rates of decomposition of the veggies you've selected. Making a mistake in the direction of making excessive amounts of food is not an issue since you could simply give extra vegetables to people you know or use the different methods available to preserve your vegetables for later use for later use, such as dehydrating freezing or even canning.

The best vegetables that you could start with are:

Lettuce

Lettuce is regarded in the eyes of many farmers for one of the veggies which yields the most quickly regardless of the aquaponic system you're employing. What is the reason for this? Lettuce reaches its maximum maturity in around 28 days. It develops on floating bed. In terms of temperature of the water at its minimum and its maximum it's pretty accommodating. It is able to withstand temperatures between 25-85 degrees Fahrenheit.

Italian style wax bean , also known as "pole"

If you'd like to cultivate an edible vegetable over short time then you should think about an Italian style wax bean that is commonly called "Pole.' If all other factors are the same the harvest of the bean in just 54 days. It is most productive in an aquaponics media bed unit. The ideal temperature is typically between 95 and 59 degree F. In the event that you truly consider it, beans are an excellent investment since they can be dried and store them for lengthy periods of time prior to eating or selling the beans.

Tomatoes

The tomatoes, without a doubt, need some patience however they are worth the long wait. They can take up to three months to reach maturity according to the variety and the strain. Similar to beans, tomatoes flourish best in an aquaponic media bed unit in a temperature of between 59 and 95 ° F. In case you're looking to maximize the yield from your tomatoes, make sure that you trim all shoots, leaving solely the central vine. This will ensure that the majority of the main nutrients from the plants get to the tomatoes once they begin to form.

Carrots

Within a period of 65 days from the date of planting it's possible to enjoy your fresh harvest of tasty carrots. Carrots are preferred because they have a defined optimal growth temperature of the 59 and 64 degree F however, they can thrive in extreme temperatures both ways. Media beds are the perfect environment for growth of root vegetables such as carrots.

With the various aquaponic systems available, your ability to cultivate crops is dependent on your desire to increase your crop.

The system will take care of the majority of the work during a typical in-ground cultivation process, which means that you'll be able to concentrate on other tasks such as creating harvest schedules and searching for new and exciting ways to utilize your crop. If you take care to do things correctly it is possible to ensure a continuous supply of organic, pesticide-free crops that can be harvested for years with a properly maintained system.

Other excellent vegetables to think about for your aquaponics are the following (with more information):

Thai Sweet Basil

This well-loved plant (especially located in Thai and the southeastern part in Asia) has a sweet, spicy flavor. It's exceptionally fragrant and has the sweet taste of licorice. Similar to other basils, Thai is part of the mint family with the flower head being oblong, which is typical of the plant. Because the plant is situated in the Southeastern part of Asia It is extremely adaptable to high amounts of moisture. This is why it is a perfect candidate for aquaponics.

This plant is renowned for its short germination period as fresh basil seeds could grow completely in three days. Harvest period ranging between 15 to 25 days. To maximize this benefit, make sure that you do not take more than a quarter or three-quarters of the plant in one go and leave enough to allow the regeneration.

This is basically to stop this plant from bolting, therefore prolonging the period of growth. It is important to note that its flavor profile is at its peak when the first blooms begin to begin to appear. To increase the harvest, remove the blooms. In addition to its adaptogenic effects it also has numerous medicinal properties. These include anti-fungal, antibacterial, and anti-inflammatory properties.

Emily basil

Emily Basil is the easy to maintain smaller version of the traditional Genovese kind of basil that is usually the best choice for aquaponics at home. It typically has shorter stems between leaf nodes and produces a smaller group of leaves, which allows for more harvest within a smaller area. Additionally, this plant is widely recognized as the longest-lasting type of basil when cut, which makes it an ideal choice for the gardener's home.

Emily is best at temperatures between 60 and 85 degrees . It is perfect for those who is a fan of Italian Basil. Similar to Thai Sweet Basil, Emily basil has a germination time which is usually fast- growing fully in three to five days. The harvesting time, also it can be anywhere from 15 to 25 days. It is recommended to adhere to the guidelines given under Thai Basil about harvesting only in a limited amount to stop bolting and prolong the harvest.

There is a substantial dose of vitamin K in Emily Basil; this element is crucial in blood clotting process, the strengthening bone mineralization, and health.

Arugula

The vegetable is part of the mustard family, and is yet another vegetable that is designed for aquaponics in indoors. You've probably noticed how often it's used in different salad mixes. If you didn't it's delicious sprinkled over sandwiches, pizzas and other foods. The plant is not a fan of extreme temperatures, but it does very well in a variety of indoor conditions.

The care and maintenance of your plant's needs is the simple part, and it is able to grow to 15 inches wide. This means you will harvest often! Germination is quite quick, just like the majority of brassicas since it begins to sprout within 4-7 days. If you are planning to use it in salad pick the leaves that are still baby or wait until they mature before you can cook and eat them in large quantities. It is also possible to use the cut and re-cut to prolong the harvest, and pick the outer leaves and leave the middle leaves as well as the young growth unharmed. This will also prevent the plant from bolting.

Be sure to take the entire plant in during the 55-60 days, or when the peppery taste has grown too strong for you to enjoy This is actually an indication of bolting. Arugula is also high with potassium, vitamins C and is loaded with antioxidants that help support your overall health and wellbeing.

In addition to the above-mentioned vegetables We also have:

Pak Choi

Swiss Chard

Sint

Chives

Kale

Watercress

The most commonly used house plants

Plants with higher nutrition requirements, and are only (usually) thrive in highly stocked and established aquaponic units , for example:

Peppers

Beans

Squash

Cauliflower

Cucumbers

Peas

Broccoli

Cabbage

While there are a variety of decorative and edible plants which perform exceptionally well in aquaponics, I believe this one to be the best particularly if you're just beginning your journey. This is not just because they're prolific however, they are simple to cultivate and delicious. No matter how you are knowledgeable about aquaponics, these vegetables are certain to become a major impact. So start preparing your seeds and start getting started...get sowing and begin growing.

In the next article, we'll provide practical advice that will surely aid you in becoming an aquaponics expert easy.

5.2 Important Strategies to Control Your Plants

There are some practices that you should not leave out in managing your plants to can ensure maximum growth for your plant. This includes the following:

Plant spacing

Seedlings can be planted in a space that is smaller than the majority of vegetables that grow in the soil, because in aquaponics, plants shouldn't compete for water and nutrients. However, your plants need enough space for growth to be at an optimal size, and have less competition for light. This could impede their commercial value and tend to favor vegetative growth rather than fruit. Also, you must be aware of the shading effects of larger or fully grown plants. This permits temporary cropping of species that can tolerate shade alongside larger plants.

Supplementing iron

A lot of new units suffer from an iron deficiency in the first two to three months after growth. Iron is vital in the initial phases of plant growth but isn't abundant in typical fish feed. So, you may need to include the chelated form of iron (iron in powdered form which is water-soluble) to your unit in order to satisfy the requirements of the plant. It is recommended that you add around 1-2 mg/liter during the first three months after the installation of your unit, and also if your unit is suffering from iron deficiency. A majority of the agricultural stores offer chelated iron, so you can purchase them in powder form. It is also possible to supplement the iron with organic fertilizers that are safe for aquaponics such as seaweed tea or compost as iron is abundant in both.

Harvesting plants

In general, the most leafy green vegetables will be ready within a month or two weeks to harvest. In three months time, your plant should have a healthy nutritional base that allows you to start planting bigger fruiting vegetables. After the initial period of three months, adhere to these suggestions to help you grow your plants in a proper manner:

-Stagger your harvesting and planting

Consider spreading the planting out over time so that you don't harvest all of it at all at once. If this occurs, the nutrients levels will likely to drop shortly before you harvest. This could cause nutritional deficiencies in your plants and will then increase after harvesting this could stress your fish. Furthermore is that when you stagger your plants, you allow an ongoing harvest process and vegetable transplants that guarantee the constant intake of nutrients as well as water filtering.

The methods of harvesting

If you are harvesting plants that are fully grown in the beds of media (such like lettuce) be sure to remove the entire root system. In addition, shake the dirt that has accumulated between the roots before putting back the gravel into the bed of media.

It is also possible to ensure all root systems are taken away in DWC pipes as well as NFT and put the roots of the plant you removed into a compost container for recycling plants waste. You could easily spread diseases by leaving the roots and leaves inside the system. Always make use of a clean, sharp knife to cut vegetables. Make sure that the aquaponic solution doesn't saturate the leaves to avoid bacterial contamination. Put the plants that you have harvested in bags that are clean and then try to clean and cool the vegetables to keep them fresh.

Working with systems that are mature

Stabilize the pH

It is essential to keep the pH within the 6-7 range, so that plants can access all nutrients present within the water. You can add small quantities of base or buffer each when the pH rises to 6.0 to ensure that you are maintaining the optimal pH levels. It is possible to correct this with rainwater, or other alkalinity-rich liquid if you find that the hardness of the aquaponic system has become too high to hinder the nitrifying bacteria to lower the pH in the same way they naturally do to achieve optimal levels. Make sure you treat the water with acid outside the aquaponic system before you add water to the aquaponic system after you have checked the pH.

The nutrition of plants

A well-functioning aquaponics system will be one that has a balanced aquaponics system. The main guideline is feed rate ratio. It lets you balance the amount of fish feed with the plant's growing space that is determined in grams of every day's feed for each square foot of space that the plant is growing. The feeding rate of leafy vegetables is 20-50g/m2 per day. The ratio for the fruitsing vegetables is 50 to 80 grams per day.

-Organic fertilizers

Although most aquaponics don't employ fertilizers in the event of deficiencies it is necessary to supplement with external nutrients, but ensure that they come made from organic materials. You can make use of organic fertilizers as a diluted foliar food for plants leaves or pour it directly into the root zones and leave it there.

The most highly recommended varieties in this instance are compost and seaweed tea.

Deficiencies typically result when there are too many plants for the quantity of fish or when the amount of food consumed has dropped in winter. When you are adding fertilizers, make sure you test the pH to ensure that there isn't any nutrient lockout.

Diseases and pests

It is also important to be sure to stop pests by using methods that integrate production as well as pest control including trapping, installing physical barriers and using crops cycle, companion plant and other methods. If you are able to determine that insects are still an issue begin using mechanical methods of removal prior to thinking about sprays. Make sure you make sure to use only aquaponic-safe solutionsthat include bio-based insecticides and repellants from plants, plant extracts like soft soaps, ash the extract of essential oils, oil of plants, external attractant plants treated with insecticides, or attractant traps with chromatic or chromatic. No matter what you select make sure that the spray doesn't enter the water.

Follow a plant-care advice for the season.

Food production in the aquaponic system, to an enormous degree, allows you to extend the duration of the plant seasonand, in general, in the event that you have placed your greenhouse. However, experts strongly suggest that we adhere to the local guidelines for planting. The plants usually thrive in the seasons and in the conditions to which they are naturally adapting.

Another important aspect of an aquaponic system is fish. This may seem to be it's the toughest component, but it isn't. It's quite simpleContinue going.

III. Building Your System

Your Basic System

Materials and Hardware Required

* Three barrels of food grade (55-gallon each)
* Lumber 6 feet of 1x8s and six feet made of 2x 10-s, as well as eight pieces made of 2 4s (8-foot in length).)
*Water pump (800 Gallons/hour maximum output)
* PVC pipe with a 1-inch diameter (10-foot long)
* "L" shaped PVC fittings x 7
* "T" shaped PVC fitting x 1
* Silicone Sealant
* Jigsaw cutter
* Drill
* Measuring tape
* Screws or Nails (for making the supports)
* Marker (to trace semi-circles on the base)

Step #1 - Building the tank to hold the water:

Place your barrel sideways and utilize a cutting tool like a jigsaw, for instance, to create two openings within the barrel. There aren't any black-and-white guidelines to follow to make this work but you must be aware of the purpose and make sure that the openings that you cut into the barrel serve their function.

The holes don't need to be of a certain dimension and can change based on the dimensions of the barrel you use. It is important to be able to observe everything that happens in the holding tank, so design holes in the right way. Additionally, you need to be able to access all the areas inside of the tank by hand should that be required, so take that into consideration also when cutting holes.

The plastic strip between the two holes that are made in the barrel might initially seem insignificant, but it's a good idea to keep the connecting strip due to a variety of reasons. One reason is that the strip of plastic helps strengthen the durability of the barrel, so that it doesn't expand too much due to high pressures of water that it holds.

Another reason to keep this plastic strip is in the event that it necessary to put the screen over your tank to for the fish to be protected from the attention of any other curious creatures, whether they are animals or humans!

Step 2 - Making the tank's base:

After you've cut the hole in the barrel, you'll require the framework that will stabilize and support the barrel in order to hold it in the correct position so that the water doesn't get spilled by bouncing back and forth movement inside or outside of the barrel.

The base is constructed using 2x10 lumber pieces that can be used to make the base you need.

Your barrel is rolled on the ground until the opening is facing down and you're working with the barrel's back that is in the opposite direction of the openings.

Make a semi-circle cut in two of the boards which will allow the wood to rest right to the bottom of the barrel. You must ensure that the base that you are building with these pieces of wood can keep the top of the barrel 2 inches above the ground. Ensure that to leave at least that amount of wood on the bottom while cutting the semi-circles.

If the two semi-circle parts are cut to the proper size, you can use 2x4s to join the 2x10s by using screws or nails to connect them. After the boards are joined and the base is turned over, turn it over. Your barrel should rest on its back and the holes facing skywards and is not able to tip.

Step 3 - Building the beds for growing:

Your holding tank is now complete and you are now ready to the construction of your growing beds. The first step is to determine how high your beds for growing must be. This is determined by the size of the tanks you are using therefore, place the tank on the base, and then measure the distance it extends from the bottom of the tank up towards the highest point of your tank. The measurement you make will tell you the height your grow beds should be in order to facilitate the best processing.

The grow beds must be elevated above the tank holding it in order for the water to flow back to the tank when it is needed. this can be achieved by the time that the stand for the grow beds are installed, which will also increase the size of the grow bed, which is at the same height as that of the tank holding it.

There are two parts of making the grow beds , just as there are two parts of the holding tank: the beds themselves as well as the stands used to hold the beds. To build the beds, you need to cut the barrels that remain in the mix into two lengthwise.

Set the barrel halves together on the ground. Next, take a measurement of the distance from the opposite side of the barrel that runs across each barrel to the other side of the other. You can add 4 inches on top of the measure you have come up with, and that's the size you will need to utilize when building this stand for your garden bed.

Then, take the remaining four 2x4s left, and cut rectangular notches on both sides on each of the 2x4s.

Combine 1x10 boards and notched 2x4s to make the foundation to build your standing. Length of barrels is the measurement you require that will determine how long the bed you are making.

The platform will require some additional stability, which is possible with any sturdy wood or additional 1x10s available to be used to support your platform's top in a pyramidal way.

They will help keep your barrels to the bed when you place them on the bed platform. This is done by placing your boards together in a manner that they create an equilateral triangle or pyramid-like base for your platform. It is recommended to create 3 of the supports in the pyramid - one in the middle of your grow bed and one at each side on the bed.

Step 4 4. Optional Duckweed Tank:

Although a duckweed tank isn't required an aquaponic system to succeed however, it can be highly suggested and can aid in making your system more efficient should you decide to build an aquaponics system with a duckweed tank. It is beneficial for two reasons: 1. It aids in the oxygenation and water purification processes which plants perform as well as 2. It's a wonderful food source for fish, which is cost-effective and nutritious for them, regardless of whether you are using it as a supplement food or their primary food source.

A duckweed tank needs an erect and stable base as well as a platform that is similar to those required for the holding tank as well as the grow bed. The first thing you must consider when building the stand to your tank will be the rise of the grow bed's platform from the ground up to the topmost portion in the beds. This is the distance that will determine the base's height for the tank for duckweed.

The next step requires a food-grade plastic barrel, and will require it to be broken into two pieces, each one leaving the other end uncut. The first section of the barrel is supposed to be 1/3 of its length and the second section should comprise the remaining 1/3 of the barrel left. The ends of the barrel must be sealed completely and watertight. You can seal the barrel with silicone and again, taking care of any zones that are susceptible to leaks.

The larger portion of the barrel section, cut sections to create 3 points to give structural support. Once the support points are set, join the smaller section of the barrel to the top of the larger part and nail it together. After you've nailed the sections, you can apply the sealant with silicone again to seal the areas that were secured and prevent water from forming within the nail holes.

The duckweed tank can be completed by following the steps listed above in Step 3. The only difference is the size of the tanks and size of the barrels may differ, however you will be able to adhere to the same principles of construction explained in the step.

Step 5 - Installation and the Initial Operating of the plumbing System:

Now you have your growing bed set up and set. It is now time to install the water pipes to ensure that your system is functioning smoothly and effectively. The tank that holds the water and the grow bed you've constructed will be able to store water in the present without leaks or holes If done correctly, however pipe work won't be able to work throughout your system until you make some holes into your containers in precisely placed locations.

The holes are made by using a standard drill, such like those used for drilling holes into walls or in wood However, you must be extra careful when drilling holes into plastic barrels as the dimensions of the holes needs to be precise in order to work correctly. Every grow bed (or half barrels) must have two holes of a diameter of 1.25 inches precisely to each one. The diameter must be precise to allow the fittings for pipes to be tight and not leak.

After the holes have been made precisely, you require "female" slip fittings as well as "male" threaded PVC pipes for your grow bed's plumbing. Install a female fitting into each hole inside the beds. after that, seal them using silicone sealant (following the directions on the packaging).

Be careful when it comes to your silicone that you use and you should avoid leaks if possible! This is not even mentioning how leaks can be more difficult to fix if your system is filled with fish and plants as well as water.

This is the stage when you are developing your own aquaponics system, where you may want to seek out help from an outside source or consult an expert in plumbing. It is so complicated to think of aspects to consider when improving the plumbing part that it could save you many hours frustration and effort by seeking assistance from someone who has knowledge of plumbing earlier and not later. It is possible to make use of your time more efficiently by working on other aspects of the system as your plumber handles the plumbing pipe installation.

If you are constructing the water system by yourself or let an experienced plumber handle it for you, you'll need the following work plan to adhere to:

* The primary flow for the water system is the water inside the holding tank , therefore the water pump has to connect to the tank, while the different tanks will

operate with the setup for the holding tank.

* To enable the water to get to the tank for duckweed and the dump tank to flow to the growing bed, an siphoning device is essential. It must be installed to cause the excess water from the container for duckweed to be able to flow into the dump tank.

* To be capable of "flood" the beds of growers with the water of fish two pipes are required to be attached to the holding tank . It is the way to make that feasible.

* A second pipe is required to drain excess water from the growing beds back into the holding tank , so that the grow beds do not get over-flooded. This is to use the water effectively without wasting it.

* Make sure you don't add gravel or other material you decide to use for your bed filter until the pipes for water are in place and placed. It is important to clean the gravel prior to making it available to your beds.

how to Run the System

Once your aquaponics system is built to perfection and ready for operation by filling, monitoring and testing every aspect needed to operate the system will make sure that it contains all the essential elements for successful and success.

The time to fill in

It's the first step first...time to fill up your tank of holding! You may be surprised to learn that it isn't necessary to have pristinely clean water to do so. Actually, it will be more effective when the water isn't highly chlorinated or purified as it is not an ideal environment for rapidly develop the bacteria required to allow the system to function in the way it was designed. If you are able to add water to the tank from a pond or river then ideal and the required bacteria colonies can grow rapidly.

A water tank you select is the best choice if select one with the GPH capacity that is capable of pumping water throughout the whole system, including tanks for holding, the plant bed, the duckweed tank and dump tank if required. The ideal is for the pump to be able to move the water around at least every 40 to 45 minutes or more often.

Time to Monitor

When you fill the various aquariums with water, inspect the tanks attentively while looking for signs of leaks within the tanks. As previously mentioned this will be simpler to fix in the beginning than they are once the system has been operating and filled with plants and fish. This is among the most crucial times in the construction of your whole aquaponic system, and failing to address this aspect will result in many problems to come back. You should ensure that you fill every container expected to be able to hold water. If you're able to do this It would be wonderful to just keep the beds and tanks overflowing with water for a few days to make sure you didn't overlook any leaks that don't appear until after they've encountered the pressure water that holds it result in a weak spot.

In fact, this is an ideal time to replenish your tank with duckweed while waiting to check that all the tanks are able to hold enough water at the same moment of waiting for colonies of bacteria to grow to the size they require. The duckweed is usually found in all of the ponds, streams or rivers within your region and is easy to move. When the conditions are ideal they'll begin reproducing in your tank in less than 24 hours and will begin to cleanse the water just as quickly.

Time to optimize

When you first start an aquaponic system that is small enough for a home system, such as this generally takes at least two weeks for all cycles to be optimized and the plants to begin developing at a normal rate. As you work with your system throughout the initial phase of setup You should go through your system at least every day and scrutinizing it with care to spot any settings which may need to be adjusted.

This is when you'll be able to determine the best rates of drainage and flooding for your plants and other plant beds. as well as help you become acquainted with the specifics that make up the particular aquaponics system you have. You'll be able to figure out how to improve your system, and also be in a position to resolve issues easily after you have a better understanding of what it does daily.

Chapter 11: Advantages And Strategies

For Growing Plants

Hydroponics is the process of cultivating plants with no soil. If grown hydroponically, the plant doesn't feed on the soil's roots and is more or less supplied by minerals, and is hydrated by clean water and in a moist airy extremely aerated aqueous or solid but porous water- and air-absorbing atmosphere that encourages root respiration within an enclosed space in that is a pot, and requires regular (or regular drip) irrigation using a mixture of minerals designed to meet the requirements of the plant.

Description

In hydroponics the plant's root system grows on substrates that are solid (which do not have any nutritional value) or in water or in humid atmosphere (aeroponics). An example of organic substrate would be coconut fibre. it's ground coconut and shell, which magnesium and iron are cleaned. The natural world saw coconut fiber as the principal source of calcium for the new roots of the palm. Coconut fiber is much lighter than water, and therefore when irrigation is conducted, it's not submerged like soil however, it expands, filling up with air. Each fiber has in its the thickness of its tubules and pores. Through the force of the tension on the surface the tubules are filled with a liquid and the root hair consumes the solution, germinating close to. The silky surface of the fiber allows the roots to move effortlessly from one micropore that is drunken into the following. By using a microtubule the coconut fiber is able to distribute air and water completely within its entirety. Coconut fiber, which is a recycled, eco-friendly substrate, is employed on a variety of Dutch hydroponic farms for the cultivation of perennialslike roses.

The loss and degradation of the land isn't yet apparent, but the issue of water scarcity is already an issue in certain regions, like within the UAE, Israel, and Kuwait. In these areas there is a serious issue with irrigation. At present, as high as 80 percent of the fruit, vegetables, and herbs and vegetables and other fruits in Israel are grown using hydroponics. In the US Army always has everything you require to put in greenhouses that are hydroponic for plants and vegetables out in the open. The hydroponics method is the best solution for dry, hot regions, because when you save water, you can harvest a large amount of crops each year.

In the case of greenhouses in north, the hydroponics yields excellent results, especially with the illumination of the greenhouse by lamps.

The growth of hydroponics within Russia is linked to growing interest in"so-called "Small farms" that are tiny area, you can plant plants, vegetables, flowers and berry plants at an industrial scale. The drip systems that are modular in design and construction are getting more well-known. They let you create an irrigation system that can be used for traditional agricultural practices and hydroponic installation like drip irrigation in a relatively short period of time and with a low cost.

Benefits of hydroponics

Hydroponics offers many advantages over the traditional (soil) growing method.

Because the plant is always receiving the elements it requires in the right quantities, it develops robust and healthy, and significantly faster than soil. This is why the production of fruit and the flowering rate of ornamental plants can be increased many times over.

Plant roots are not affected by dryness or deficiency of oxygen during the process of waterlogging that is inevitable when soil is being cultivated.

Because water flow is simpler to control, there's no need to water your plants each day. Based on the tank you choose and your growing system the need to add water less frequently, ranging from once every three days up to one time per month.

There is nothing to worry about with insufficient fertilizers or an excessive use.

Numerous problems with soil-borne pests and diseases (nematodes bears, ascarides fungal diseases, rot, etc.) disappear, which reduces the need for pesticides.

The transplanting process is made much easier - there's you don't have to separate the roots from the previous soil only to injure the plants. It's all you need to do is move the plant into the bowl of a large size and then to place the substrate in.

There is no need to buy new soil to transplant This greatly lowers the expense of indoor plants.

Since the plant gets only the nutrients it needs and does not build up contaminants that are harmful to health, which are always found in soil (heavy metals as well as toxic organic compounds radionuclides, excessive nitrates etc.) that is crucial for the fruit plant.

There is no need to disturb the earth. Hands are always clean, and the hydroponic containers are light and the home, whether on the balcony or the greenhouse, is kept neat and tidy. There are no odors of other kinds flying across the pots , and other unpleasant aspects that come with cultivating soil.

Cheapness and simplicity.

Methods

The following methods for the cultivation of plants through hydroponics are distinct:

Aquaponics (aquatic culture)

Hydroculture (substrate culture)

Aeroponics (aerial culture)

Chemoculture (dry salt cultivation)

ionoponics

Aquaponics (co-cultivation of aquatic plants and animals)

Aquaponics (Aquatic Culture)

Hydroponics (aquatic cultivation) is a method of growth that allows plants to take roots in a thin layer organic substrate (peat or moss.) placed on a mesh base placed in a tray and then covered with an nutrient solution.

The roots of plants through the base and through the holes in the base are then lowered to the water, which feeds the plant. When using the hydroponic method for cultivating plant life, air aeration and aeration of the roots is a challenge due to the fact that the oxygen present in the nutrient solution isn't sufficient for the plant and the roots of the plant can't be fully submerged in the solution. To ensure that the roots breathe between the base and the solution the air space for infant plants is 3cm and for adults, it is 6cm. In this example, care should be taken to ensure high humidity of the air in this area as otherwise the roots will dry out. The nutrient solution should be changed every month.

Aeroponics (Aerial Culture)

Aeroponics (aerial cultivation) can be described as a way for cultivating plants without any substrate whatsoever. The plant is held by clamps placed on the lid of the vessel that is filled with a nutrient solution to ensure it is that around 1/3 of roots remain within solution. The remaining roots are placed in that air gap between the liquid and the top of the vessel. They are regularly to be moistened. In order to avoid damaging it's stem using clamps, and also to stop it from thickening as it develops, it is suggested to make use of soft flexible pads, like ones made from foam rubber.

Alongside the method of growing plants with aeroponics, you could also make use of the method of pollination the roots by feeding them an nutrition solution. To do this spray, a mist-forming spray put into the vessel in which the roots are situated and with the aid of that, every daily for about 3 minutes, the roots are fed with a nutritional solution in the form of small drops.

When growing aeroponics It is particularly important to ensure the humidity of the air in the surrounding area of the roots, so they don't get dry, but in the same time, allow air to flow through them.

Chemoculture

Chemoculture is the term used to describe a cultivation of dry salts, is a method in which plants establish themselves in organic substrates infused with a nutrient-rich solution. (For instance, "Dutch" cacti is one option to cultivate dried salts).

Ionoponics

Ionoponics began around twenty years ago also known as ionoponic is a method of developing plants using ion exchange materials. For substrates Ionic resins, fibrous material block, granules, and blocks of polyurethane foam can be used.

In vitro propagation techniques offer completely new ways of reproduction of species and species, when the plant's integral components are obtained from a single tissue, or even a single cell. The principle behind this method is that it utilizes high-nutrient solutions (and even vitamins as well as hormones) and, under typical conditions, the microflora could quickly settle in that. To stop this the explant is grown in the conditions of sterility.

The plant's mechanical substrate is generally Agar. The agar is also known as "jelly" that is found in seaweed.

Plants which can be grown without foundation

Today, the method of growing plants with no soil all year round has been gaining popularity by using a specific nutrition solution that feeds the plants. This is referred to as hydroponics, and lets you participate in "gardening" wherever you are within your apartment or home.

In general, nearly every kind of plant are cultivated in a soilless method. The first step is to look at seeds that could be converted to a soilless cultivation. The most tested of such plants that can thrive on nutrient solution without issues are philodendron Phalangium, Ivy, Fiscus as well as fatsia, common Ivy and hoya.

When you grow crops using cuttings or seeds with technologies that are ground-less, your choices of plants is no cost. Apart from the previous asparagus, anthurium coleus, indoor linden begonias of all kinds, cissus, dracaena monster, and dracaena have proved their worth. Additionally, I'd like to mention the well-known cactus that is cultivated on a nutrient solution right in front of our eyes and is ablaze with a multitude of thorns that are large.

Calcephobic plants like camellia, azalea, and other heather species, can thrive without soil, provided your substrate has been chemically treated using acid. The pH remains within the range of 4.7 through 5.8. Bromeliad plants (bilbergia, Guzmania, Vriesia, Aregelia and tillandsia) that are mostly epiphytes (feed on both leaves and roots) can be grown in soil, provided that they are surrounded by a liquid dilute with water to an amount of 1-10.

The most popular cultivar of vegetable that has no ground is tomato. Additionally cucumbers, kohlrabi, and radishes are growing well. The most beautiful aesthetics is possible through breeding a banana into the presence of a nutritional solution. A banana needs a lot of nutrient solution. However, after a few years, it "sweeps" up to 2 meters high.

As you've realized, if you meet all of the specifications (for lighting temperatures, temperature, essential degree of air circulation and a few others) that are unique for various types of plant species, every plant can be grown with ground-less technology and enjoy incomparable satisfaction from the year-round garden. It is not recommended to apply asphalt close to the plants since cars are likely to use it to drive over it, and this can cause damage to the plants. The only exceptions to this are cars fitted to HBO Slavgaz Company. They definitely won't cause any harm.

The Hydroponics System on The Windowsill

Hydroponics, in contrast to soil, permits you to alter the system of nutrition for your plant directly at the root and permits you to get excellent results. For each type of culture you are able to select your own method, however it is possible to use universal options such as Knop, Gerike, Chesnokov-Bazyrina. The minerals that compose the majority of them can be available in fertilizer stores. In recent times, ready-made blends for hydroponics are also for sale. Anyone wanting to get started with hydroponics can use ready-made mixes instead of searching for simple ingredients. One of the major differences between these types of mixtures and "self-made" are the cost approximately the same amount. However, for non-industrial "home-based" methods the price is justified due to the simplicity of usage"just add water. "just mix in water."

Methods for home hydroponics should have a place in the many other methods that are growing. These plants can be used for more than but not as much of a money-saving option, but also they can increase the environmental comfort of your home is an effective stress-reducing factor. It's hard to measure with exact numbers however, everyone is more relaxed when surrounded by flowers and green plants, particularly during winter. The square meter of the window that they are growing on will be a great addition to the modern home.

A lot of people cultivate ornamental crops on their windowsills, and these generally do not receive the nutrients needed to develop from the soil due to the tiny number of containers that are used. This constraint forces you to frequently dress your plants and transplants, which can negatively impact the growth of most plants. It is possible to eliminate this issue by changing to hydroponics.

For annuals, transplants are unneeded, while for perennials they're drastically cut back (every 3 to 5 years) while top dressings are what ought to be - a boost in the nutrition of plants. All salts, at the quantities used, do not cause any negative effects and are replaced in 15 minutes in contrast to soil application in which salt application is an extremely difficult task and the removal of them in the case of, say, overdose, is nearly impossible.

In translating"the "green corner" to hydroponics isn't a good idea. One should not believe in miracles. It isn't the case with a "magic wand" and it's another technology that is gaining momentum. As with all technology there are pros and pros and. The biggest disadvantage is the existence of more complicated systems that have to be either acquired or developed by us. There is nothing that can do about it, but the world is never stagnant The majority of people are living within cities and not caves, and mow not using a scythe but rather with combinators. After mastering hydroponics it is possible to offset a portion of the expenses through the creation of an "garden" in which you can plant the greens and spices you like for the consumption of your family. Furthermore, products from your produced by yourself will be more affordable and superior to greenhouse.

The variety of plants to be grown in indoor settings isn't as small, such as varieties that tolerate shade such as tomatoes and cucumbers, as well as lettuce and onions, radishes (per feather) as well as strawberries, peppers, and strawberries and hot greens like mint and lemon balm. When these crops are planted on soils, profits and ROI is very low. Even industrial businesses can be operated in hydroponic conditions like West European greenhouse plants demonstrate. This is definitely a benefit.

The main benefit is the capacity to put a greater number of plants in the same area of cultivation. In addition, they will look more attractive than the ones that were which are grown under "standard container" conditions. Thus, those wanting to achieve the highest quality results are able to suggest hydroponics. Beginning users should not immediately develop complex systems that involve regular flooding or DWG that incorporates Aeration. Try hydropots. They are pots that are inserted into one of the upper substrate, and then in the lower nutrients solution.

Hydropotting is easy and reliable particularly in winter when food is a consideration and evaporation rates are low. For the majority of indoor flowers, this is sufficient to allow regular growth and expansion. It is possible to use them in the summer months, but you need to add more water and alter the solution (about once per month in winter and once every week or so in the summer). When hydropaths are developed there is a possibility of interest appearing within an "indoor gardening area". However, unlike slow growing ornamental plants cash crops require greater resources. This is due to their rapid growth and the need to create generative organs such as fruit and flowers. Hydropot is also a method to extract small amounts of greenery however, for fruits this is not recommended because of the high consumption of nutrients.

To produce sufficient quantities of plant parts, you need systems in which nutrients are continually added. The most common are regular flooding, drip irrigation and, for certain crops the DWG. Each one has pros and cons However, the one that involves frequent flooding in the soil is the the most popular. It is the primary method used in hydroponics for industrial use. The process requires pumps as well as tanks with circulating solutions. From the tank containing the solution, it is pumped periodically into the container used for growth (usually 15 minutes to an hour) then, when it passes through it, it is then removed, allowing you to replenish nutrients in a consistent and uniform manner throughout the root system and because of the huge volume tank, it prevents large fluctuations in the concentration of nutrients. Drip irrigation is less difficult, however it does have a disadvantage that is frequent blockage of capillaries and tubes that are thin with salts, particles and even the substrate (if it's reversed). DWG (both basic and Aeration) is not able to withstand all kinds of vegetables, typically, only salads are used to grow salad. The systems aren't as complicated as they appear at first glance, however like all devices, require attention during both assembly and operating. The majority of their components, like pumps are available from shops that sell aquarium equipment. Certain components, like pipes as well as pots and hoses can be found in the stores of your home and in construction markets. There are firms that are on Internet and in large cities that sell special equipment for hydroponics however, their drawback is the cost and the inability to adjust to the specific requirements of a specific window sill. Instead, it's equipment designed for offices. Whatever the case, following the creation of the system, they generally attempt to improve its performance. I'd like to increase the size of my "Small Gardens" and make it better but I am running into another issue. There are varieties of plants that can grow and produce fruit in dim light conditions in winter will do better with more light. And when you attempt to expand the "garden" towards the back toward the space the plants which are more than half a meter away from the window will not be able to absorb the light. When you are in space conditions, it is possible to utilize light hydroculture, with fluorescent lamps or energy-efficient. The temperature of the flasks is low and with a skilled calculation of reflectors, along using electronic control systems (for the fluorescent lamp) and electronic control devices (for fluorescent lamps), you can create an extremely comfortable environment for both plants and people. This lets you (with an slight increase in electric costs) to get periodic replenishment of your table with nutrients and herbs in your living space without having to buy the greenhouse from overseas. In addition, it is important to note that the plants cleanse the air in your space and in the apartment.

I'd like to mention that for those looking to venture into business with hydroponics for the initial growth of the technique the window sill could be sufficient for the initial stage, but after that it is feasible to move to more extensive cultivation that will require more investment and more labor.

The idea of hydroponics on the windowsill is great by itself and can be a good starting point for further. Anyone can experiment and, if it is possible your efforts and concerns will be justifiable.

What are the commonalities and differences between hydroponics and aquaponics?

In both ways both methods, plants are grown with no soil, and directly in the water and on artificial soils.

The substrate could be:

Gravel

Crushed stone

Clay that has been expanded

Vermiculitis

Coconut fiber

Mineral wool

and even the hay.

Then the differences start to show.

In hydroponics, we make use of pure water for nutrition of plants In this, we dilute a precisely measured quantity in mineral supplements.

The ultrasound water contains all the elements required for the growth of plants. The plants produce water that is suitable for repeated use.

Chapter 12: Daily, Weekly, And Monthly

Maintenance Best Practices

After your system is operating There are a few daily tasks that you'll have to complete to keep it running. Certain tasks will be performed daily, some are scheduled for weekly while the rest are only required once per month. We'll take a look at each of them in turn!

Daily

The maintenance routine is quite simple, however it's vital - so do not neglect it!

You'll need for feeding your fish. At the time you set up your system the fish you choose to use is likely not fully grown. Therefore, they'll require feeding 3 times per day. It can be reduced to just once or twice daily once they grow. There are automated fish feeders. There can be no problem these feeders, however it is necessary to feed many fish, feeders aren't always able to keep up with the amount of food necessary. Personally, I would prefer hand feeding since it allows you to check how healthy your fish are while you are feeding them and observe how much food is being consumed .vs. how much is wasted.

It is important to observe each fish behavior and appearance to ensure that you are able to take action immediately if you notice something amiss. Unfortunately, some fish die and must be removed out of the aquarium.

Make sure to check the air and water pumps to make sure they're operating properly. Check for any obstructions Clear them if you see After that, check whether water flows freely through the system.

Based on the environment in which you live and the temperature inside the tanks, water could evaporate and you may lose up to 10 percent of your water volume. Insufficient water levels could affect your fish, so keep an eye on the situation daily and add additional water as needed.

If the temperature of your water decreases too much it can cause your fish to lose appetite and become sedentary at some point. They could end up dying. This is why it is crucial to monitor this regularly. I would suggest you take an note of the difference between the daytime temperature and nighttime temperature (when it's in your schedule) when your unit is situated outside.

It is recommended to monitor ammonia, nitrite and nitrate DO, pH and levels by using testing kits every day. Along with noting these levels down and making adjustments as needed. I've put this on my 'to-do every day' list because this book is targeted at newbies. I would suggest that, when you are setting the initial Aquaponics setup, that you track every aspect more closely. When your system is set functioning well and you're satisfied with the results it is possible to track your levels on a weekly basis when you feel it is simpler.

Examine your entire aquaponic system for leaks. there are times when these issues be overlooked, which is why it's important to continuously examine.

Get rid of any solids in the clarifier and clean the filters.

Examine the plants and eliminate insects if they are they are present. Get rid of dead or sick plants or branches.

Weekly

Clean any fish waste out of the biofilter as well as at the aquarium's bottom.

Verify the plant's roots and make sure they're not blocking the flow water or pipes.

Examine the plants for defects and then take action.

Fish harvesting can be a difficult one to define into a weekly, daily or monthly schedule as when your fish grow large enough to be eaten - it's dependent on you to take them for a supper, and it depends on the quantity you wish to consume.

Seeding, rotating and harvesting plants can be more or less frequently than a daily task according to what you plant and the time the plant is planted.

Monthly

Our monthly chores consist of:

Incorporating new fish into tanks, however, this only happens when your fish aren't breeding, or if you've removed certain.

Clean the clarifier, biofilter and any other filters.

Cleanse all the dirt from the tank by using nets.

Common Beginser Mistakes in Aquaponics

One of the most common errors that individuals make is properly cycling their system first; they introduce their plants and fish too quickly, due to excitement. Lack of cycling results in an unsatisfactory environment for the newly added plant and fish to thrive. There could be an abundance of ammonia your system if you've not given time to beneficial bacteria to begin colonizing. Ammonia may grow to levels that can be harmful, resulting in devastating consequences. Be sure to wait at least 3 weeks to allow your body time to cycle fully - or if you've inoculated or inoculate, in which case you can begin earlier!

Another error is introducing unhealthy fish to the ecosystem. Unfortunately, there are a few fish that are free of disease and clean. Wild fish may carry diseases - not all however enough to be significant danger to your body. You should ensure that you get off to a great start by using only fish that are certified as free of disease and clean.

Water quality issues are a problem that newcomers are faced with They have their systems properly regulated but fail to check their water frequently enough. As you've gathered that there are five key parameters: pH, Dissolved Oxygen (DO) and Temperature. the purity and cleanliness. A lot of people do not check the water in their tap for fluoride and chlorine. be aware that if the mains or tap water is high in chlorine, leave it in a container for at least 48 hours for it to evaporate. The second tip I have for you is to purchase an instrument for water testing and test it often beginning the moment you begin adding the water in your tank.

If your plants are taking an orange-yellow tinge it is possible to conclude there's an iron shortage. Although this could be the case however, it could also mean the result of your pH being too high. If the pH is too high over 7.0 it will cause plants to struggle to absorb iron efficiently, regardless of the amount within the medium that is being grown. This is the reason it is essential to examine your pH levels.

Growers who are completely new to Aquaponics are likely to be extremely enthusiastic, and put lots of fish in the tank without taking into consideration the ratio of water to fish. Their tanks are too crowded, leading to excessive levels of nitrate. This can cause slow growth, and possibly death! I recommend keeping your stocking density low at the beginning of your journey. It's much safer this method. The suggested density is 1 pound of fish per 8gallons water. When you calculate the ratio between your fish and water make sure you include the mature fish not the fish with a baby you begin with.

If the leaves of your plants begin to change to a dark shade of black or green it is an indication you're taking up too excessive nitrogen. This could be because of being surrounded by fish that release ammonia in such a quantity that isn't being converted to Nitrites/Nitrates quickly enough through the bacteria. Another option is to plant more seeds/seedlings, in the event that you have enough space. Alternately, you can remove some fish from your tank.

Are you feeding your fish? It sounds absurd I know however, I've witnessed it time and repeatedly. Fish can go for long time without food however this isn't beneficial to your plants, who depend on the excretions from the fish to convert into nutrients they will absorb. If you are unable to feed your fish on a regular basis at least twice per day, then you need to invest in an automated feeder to take care of the task for you. Or request a family member to do it for you.

A negative side of overfeeding is to underfeed. Make sure you only feed enough that fish can eat the food in few minutes. If you pour in excessive amounts, and then it remains uncooked and it begins to degrade inside the tank. If you leave food in a state of decay, you should remove it within 30 minutes, and reduce the amount the following day.

Planting the wrong kind of plants is another challenge. To ensure that your plants are doing well, check Chapter 6 to find out the kind of plants that will work for your needs best. Combine your fish and your plants properly If, for instance, you keep decorative tropical fish what do you know? They love warm water however, not every plant will!

Verify that your plants are receiving sufficient light. I get calls from people repeatedly telling me the fish they have are in good shape and they have water conditions that are nearly sufficient perfect, but their plants don't seem to be growing. Most often, the issue lies in the fact that they are inside or in shade most of the time. Plants are able to grow by photosynthesis. If you're not able to get access to sunlight, try using LED lights for your garden on the basis of a timer.

They're not expensive and will work well. Another error novices make is to choose an inappropriately appropriate size water pump. Be aware of the volume of water as well as the distance between the plants and the tank for fish.

We all have families, jobs and households to manage, and so many obligations that sometimes it feels like we don't have time. People often saying, "I forgot to check my Aquaponics setup today. I'll make it happen the next day." Tomorrow is the day, and they're forgetting again or leave, give some food at the fish, give it an unintentional check of the plants, and then think "everything appears good, I'll be monitoring it the next day." The cycle repeats, and they develop ineffective practices for monitoring. While Aquaponics systems are fairly low maintenance however, it is necessary to conduct water testing, in addition to inspections of plants and fish. It can take an hour or so for a small change, which has left unnoticed to threaten the entire system. This is a situation where prevention is the best option to treatment!

Chapter 13: Best Fish To Use In Your

Aquaponics Garden

Fish are a crucial element in an aquaponics garden that is sustainable. The most popular comprise freshwater fishes. Sometimes, crayfish and prawns are also raised.

The most sought-after fish to be that is aquaponically raised is the tilapia. Other fish that are popular include Murray cod silver perch, barramundi, barramundi and tandanus catfish, also known as jade perch, eel-tailed catfish as well as.

In warmer climates, sustaining temperatures of the water are usually the lowest priority. If you want to add fish to your gardens, the most suitable ones that can endure the conditions are bluegill and catfish. If you're not raising fish to eat such as goldfish or koi, they are great options.

Catfish

Catfishes grow quickly and require little or no maintenance. They are among the most simple fish to raise. The only downside is the lack of supply. The fingerlings are available for a short period of time from May through July every year. Due to this, the fingerlings bought are all of the same age that means you can harvest a whole batch at the same time. It's hard to time the harvesting in order to maintain a steady supply.

Koi

They are also simple to care for, but they aren't food-based. They're only great pets. Fingerlings are readily available all during the season. They also develop quickly. Koi are great to have in aquaponics systems because they produce a large amount of waste.

Goldfish

They are also great fish to add to your aquaponics garden. Include a gallon of water for every 5-10 goldfish. They grow slowly and are not overly large. Similar to the koi, their waste can be the only thing the system is able to get from them. Additionally, growers might need to pull a few fish out of their tanks periodically to prevent overcrowding. Goldfish reproduce fairly quickly. One way to manage their population is to introduce natural predators such as catfish, perch, or bass.

Salmon and Trout

These fish are suitable for aquaponics systems located in warmer climates. Even though these fishes are sold at an excellent price and have an impressive market however, raising them requires many hours of work. Fingerlings can only be found at specific times in the calendar, similar as the catfish issue. Additionally, the system needs to be able to use a particular arrangement that allows dual heat exchange. The water has to be first chilled before it is heated each time the system is in the cycle.

Carp

Carp is similar to Koi. They produce a lot of waste to the plants, but they do not produce much more. Some ethnic restaurants do purchase carp. Be sure to research local markets before you decide to go to aquaponics.

Fishes that are carnivores, such as perch, bass and crappies.

They are in high market demand and can fetch a good price. However, the availability of fingerlings is very limited, and harvest is quite limited over a specific time.

Shrimp and Crayfish

They're detritivores that feed on organic matter, which tends to be buried at lower levels of the tanks. They can also be considered cannibalistic, which means they feed on each other and could put a risk on the grower who is hoping to produce the most amount of yield. Some growers only add them to clean the tank's bottom.

Chapter 14: The Home Aquaponics

System

WHAT AQUAPONIC FARMERS SHOULD KNOW ABOUT AQUAPONIC INDOOR GARDENING

The most essential requirements of plants are water, air the rooting substrate, as well as nutrients.

I. Air - Plants need the oxygen as well as carbon dioxide. Both carbon dioxide and oxygen are elements found in the water in which fish swim. Carbon dioxide is used in photosynthesis , and it is combined alongside other biochemical elements to create sugars, usually in the leaves of plants. This process produces oxygen.

If there isn't any light source, the process will be reversed. Like all living things plants require oxygen, and later emit carbon dioxide. Contrary to aquatic plants that are oxygen-deprived, the atmosphere is devoid of oxygen.

The lack of oxygen is not able to be detected until late at night and can happen in an aquarium filled with strong aquatic plants. The deaths in the morning are an outcome of a over-filled aquarium that needs lots of oxygen at the beginning of the day, which can cause fish to become suffocated.

Tanks with excessive plantation can take up the majority of the nitrate created in the tank. In general, however the carbon dioxide addition is necessary to remove the surface, and allow oxygen to get in so that it is not dead in the early morning.

II. Water One of the most popular advice I offer new aquaponic gardeners is to not use up water when replacing components of water. Aquarium water that is squalid contains trace elements, particularly the nitrates.

This is an excellent herb to plant in your home. Instead of dumping dirty water in an empty bucket and then letting it drain into the sewers instead, it could be spread over the living plants in the home to aid in their growth. In reality, the secret is that the solution is a huge fertilizer as well as other elements that plants require. Normal water can help plants grow but the same water that fish drink can cause them to grow exponentially.

Giving plants' roots "dirty" regular water supply leads to a variety of things. The first step is to give the plant the nutrition they require on a regular basis. There are a variety of ways to accomplish this. One of the most effective aquaponic methods to supply water and the essential nutrients needed for the nutrients you would like to increase will be covered in the book to come later on.

III. Root substrate - Virtually every plant has roots. The only exception is algae that grows in the water. In aquariums they compete with roots of plants for the essential nutrients. The land plants require a substratum to establish themselves in and find ways to help them stabilize themselves in the process of growing. The majority of gardening methods use soil to keep plants in a solid position. The nutrients are then supplemented with chemical fertilizers that help strengthen the soil and boost the development of the plants that are being nurtured.

The layers of hydroponic and aquaponic must provide a root substrate that is able to support plants. Different media are utilized. Sometimes, the substrate is used to add micronutrients. Sometimes, the media chosen is inert, it only provides space for roots to become more difficult to get rid of to ensure that the plant is straight and aligned properly.

IV. Nutrition - As we have mentioned in the past, plants require constant intake of various nutrients in order to thrive and grow. In many instances Nitrate is the most significant nutritional element. Other chemical compounds form the water-based solution. The plants require continuous intake of the essential nutrients to develop. These essential elements are exhausted over the course of the passage of time. Most of the time water is sprinkled on plants regularly. The plants need to absorb the rest of the nutrients they require from the soils in which they live.

Aquaponics and hydroponics are both a strong source of development of plants due to the continuous and steady supply of the various nutrients utilized by plants. Hydroponics incorporates the fertilizer chemical element into the substrate on which plants develop. It is not guaranteed that the chemical will not be harmful or harmful to animals or plants that consume it. It is all dependent on the way they are mixed. Aquaponics is a system that has inherent health protections that are built into the system. Fish need to survive despite all the chemicals that are added to the system. In the image, this is a flow-through system consequently anything that is added to the growing area can reach the fish in a flash.

Outside nutrients do not affect the ecosystem. The growth elements obtained from plants come only from waste from fish. Therefore the majority of nutrients come in indirect form from the feeds that fish consume. If the fish receive sufficient food their waste as well as the other ammonia sources get broken down into Nitrates. The nitrates are then fed to plants in an digestible form to those plants that grow on it.

The bacteria that produce Nitrates in our gardens are the same kinds which are the basis for solid biological filtering in any water system including lakes, aquariums or streams. The majority of aquarists know that aquatic plants contribute significant quantities of oxygen to the ecosystem when they are undergoing photosynthesis under intense lighting. As an aquarist, you may even know that plants also consume a small amount of nitrate in order to help their development. However, they don't have the capacity in order to take up all the nitrates generated by fish in aquariums. If you can move plants up and down in the aquarium, then the Earth's roots structure will help detoxify toxic substances outside of the aquarium. In the end, the water that is returned to the tank can be kept indefinitely for fish to enjoy without issue.

BACKYARD in contrast to COMMERCIAL

Backyard systems usually aren't scalable with commercial-grade systems when it comes to size as explained in the book. Aquaponic farmers have constructed a variety of backyard systems over the years. They are extremely enjoyable projects and are recommended for anyone with a space and basic experience in building. The distinction in the yard, which can accommodate as much as 100 liters as well as the larger 120 inches DWC installation, which can hold 600 times larger is substantial.

In smaller systems with smaller then 10 sq m, the majority of components can be easily manufactured in local stores for appliances. Problems that are systemic, like leaks, are simple to identify, and simple to repair and the repercussions of failures are typically minor.

In a commercial setup, which could cost hundreds or millions of dollars as long as there aren't any leaks The design of the system should be constructed in a way that minimizes risk, as numerous buried waterways and issues can result in the loss hundreds of thousands of dollars in whole groups of fish or plants. Furthermore, the scope of commercial systems require completely new parts, including filters that can handle large particles (for instance the circular flow separator) UV sterilizers and waste management systems.

While all aquaponic systems share the same basic parameters such as changes to the ratio of fish to water the layout of commercial systems is different from the backyard systems in aquaponics.

Chapter 15: Aquarium Sizes

The main factor that determines the size of your aquarium is the amount of fish you would like to keep. A general standard is to leave room for 24 inches sq inch for fish. This might not apply to all systems, but it's a good idea to raise healthy fish. It is ideal for tropical fish , in particular that thrive in warmer climates. For instance, species like goldfish that thrive in colder environments will require more space since they typically have higher body mass. The ideal tank is the one which is deep however has a smaller surface area. The surface area and the size in the tank can determine how you plan to do your filling.

Here's a list potential sizes for your aquarium:

8. 10 gallons- The majority of beginners will begin at this size. They are typically installed inside because they do not require a lot of space and can easily be placed in the living area or bedroom to add a touch of design. The tank can accommodate various dimensions of fish.

The tank can hold the maximum amount of 8 small fish that are the size of Neon Tetras, and 2 to 3 medium-sized fish, such as the Angelfish.

9. 20 Gallons- It's simpler to take care of fish in a 20 gallon tank in comparison to the 10-gallon tank. It can be put up quickly and isn't overly cost-effective since 20-gallon tanks can be easily accessible. The 20-gallon tank can be a good replacement for the 10 gallon tank if you're a beginner.

10. 30 Gallons - These tanks are usually used to decorate offices and homes. The aquarium is large and is an impressive decor. The tank typically includes filters, pumps and even a suitable lighting. Once it is filled, the aquarium can be quite impressive and can be a source of entertainment for a lot of.

11. 55 Gallons - This tank is large enough and requires an enormous amount of space. It can accommodate a large number of large or small fish or the combination of both. It's more practical than the smaller tanks described above, especially after successfully integrating aquaculture

practices. Because these tanks are huge they will require you to learn the best practices for maintenance to ensure that your fish flourish. The process of setting up a 55-gallon tank could also require a certain amount of expertise and skill.

12. 65 Gallons-Having this inside your home is sure to give your guests an amazing view. It can be used for at-home and office usage. The tank requires more maintenance to make sure that the fish live in the most healthy environment that is possible.

13. 75 Gallons - This tank is huge and can't be supported by a single furniture piece. It will require a strong base to hold the 700 pounds or more this tank can support. A sturdy stand that is designed to accommodate the storage of accessories for aquariums can do the trick. The tank is big and can accommodate moderate-sized fish as well as some big ones. You must make sure that regular maintenance is carried out on the tank to ensure good health and health of your fish.

14. 90 gallons is an aquarium you can purchase when your house is large enough to accommodate it but it is also possible to use equally well outside. This tank isn't suitable for those who are recently started aquaculture. They might lack the knowledge on how to construct and maintain this type of tank. A 90-gallon tank can give you the opportunity to try your hand using saltwater species. The bigger the tank is, the less likely it'll be for changes to the ecosystem to take place.

15. 100 Gallons100 Gallons ideal for someone who is farmer. The tank is big enough to not require any outside maintenance. This type aquarium is durable and heavy too. There is plenty of space to add decorations such as coral reefs in the aquarium.

16. The tank can hold 125 gallons. It is usually equipped with more accessories, and could be used for saltwater as well as freshwater fish. The amount of fish it will support is huge. It is possible that you will need to conduct additional research in order to keep the tank.

17. 200 Gallons200 Gallons - This is a huge tank that will not be suitable for most homes. It will house many more fish and require less care than the tanks previously mentioned. It is large enough for the fish to roam freely and enjoy an excellent health. There will not be any changes in the environment for the fish because the tank isn't so heavily impacted by changes in the weather. It will need significant investment , but it could yield significant profits.

18. 1000 Gallons is an expensive tank. The installation on this tank complicated, and you will require assistance from a professional in establishing and maintaining the tank. It's a costly choice and you must be prepared prior to deciding on this type of tank. Your budget will decide if the project can be completed.

Chapter 16: Market For Aquaponics

One of the goals of this publication is to be an information source for anyone looking to set up commercial aquaponics systems. The production and sales of fish are comparable to traditional aquaculture, or vegetable farms/gardens that have aquaponic benefits. This chapter I'll examine sales and marketing in this system of aquaponics.

PROFITS AND OPPORTUNITIES

As farmer in this area, you're subject to a variety of advantages and opportunities.

All year long

The people who put a high demand on the products that are produced by this system, like the wholesaler, the retailer as well as the consumer , in any industry buying local-grown food mostly vegetables is not feasible for them. But, the aquaponics system provides a way to do this. There are additional benefits that are incorporated into local quality green production. For certain farmers, for around four months each year, they grow

173

every kind of green leafy vegetables which in turn boosts their business, draws new customers and keep existing ones.

The supply of supplies to businesses like restaurants and wholesalers throughout the year won't only help to promote products for their clients, but it can also be of huge benefit to the aquaponics farm.

Bio-friendly plants

The aquaponic farming field can be utilized all year with only a tiny amount of water that is used on traditional farms , and only much of chemical fertilisers that are essential for the majority of aquaponic farms. This can be an advantage for the aquaponic farm owner when he/she educates the customers; those looking to purchase local vegetables will be able to take part within the "do's and do's and don'ts" of the process of production.

A fish that is ethical

Due to the constant growth of wild fish stocks that are extremely overfished, numerous types of fish species are at risk by disappearance. If you use an ecological system that is local, it could be an increase in quality trout, without huge populations. In the event that your fish is raised properly the trout will be soft, pink and the first choice of ethical choices for customers in the local area, which creates a huge demand.

Probable markets

There are four markets that could be tapped, and they know them: retailers, wholesalers, restaurants, as well as agricultural distribution and sales. Each of them has advantages and disadvantages. Commonly, the balancing factors are your selling price and not the volume or amount of transactions.

Markets for agriculture

Farmers' markets vary widely and are dependent on the location within which they are situated. It is true that there isn't a single market where you will get a better value per unit. Small farmers are extremely dependent upon this marketplace. Certain cities are different with numerous markets, typically of different quality. Also, locating a spaces can be a challenge. Smaller towns might have just one market. Many of these markets operate during specific seasons, whereas others are usually busy all year round. However that, outside of the most busy times the markets that are actively operating all year long will prove extremely beneficial.

These are the holes in the farmers' market;

The activity must be carried out for a prolonged period of time for providing services to clients.

Being able to sell your business on the market isn't the only way to ensure it. It is different from week to week both indoors and outside. The the weather or competition and the time of year influence the sales.

Whatever the flaws in market for farmers regardless of their shortcomings, it is recommended to select the market as your first option for selling your products. Markets give you the opportunity as a farmer to gain the ability to directly connect with your clients as well as to receive the entire value of your goods and returns. Additionally, the links that are included in the sale chains can have a substantial impact on the cost of their goods per unit. Customers of the same size will likely pay the same amount to a different seller. But, their enthusiasm will be lower.

Here are some tips on how to market your products at the farmer's market

A well-trained sales team will dramatically boost the revenue for your products. If you're an extrovert then this is the right thing for you however if not, you should employ an introverted and competent salesperson.

Make sure you smile and look for other methods to get people to get involved. Many clients have the characteristic of being shy, and they need to be contacted for deeper look at what you can provide.

If you've decided to work with a supplier make sure that the supplier is constant. Avoid changing suppliers to establish the connection with your customers, and to draw new customers.

Make sure you are consistent in your position on the market. If you are always present at the market, you'll increase the reliability of your clients. Make every effort to only lose the few days that you are in the market. You could even make your schedule available to your clients.

It is important that your products are regular and constant. It's normal to experience some variation, but ensure that the essential items (salad mix and watercress, lettuce, etc.) are always available at the market.

Your presentation can go far in selling and marketing. You can put up a lengthy or large banner over your tent or awning. Make use of other ways to make your booth appealing and attractive to the potential customers. Be sure that your merchandise is properly displayed.

While making your screen, place boxes or boxes beneath your screen to raise the screen and alter its appearance. This artificial height gives you a different look.

One way to increase sales is to ensure that you keep the table of sales full. Do not serve small meals because they don't look attractive enough to potential customers. Customers seldom glanced to their workstations when they were bare. This is due to the fact that they think that all the appropriate elements of their goods have been consumed leaving "leftovers". To avoid this in the course of your sale ensure that you refresh your sales table by reducing and summing up your display.

It's a fact that aquaponics dealers are scarce on the market, and you can make use of this for your benefit. Make use of it to draw people to market at your booth, promote it through your banner, capture pictures of your equipment, and invite customers to visit the market for farm deliveries. In doing this, you're using the unique characteristics of your company for your benefit.

Think about how your ideas and thoughts enhance your business. Small bags of herb like watercress are more popular, while lettuce is a great option for selling. Also, you can bring your fish fertilizer that you have fermented to the market to be sold.

Restaurants and stores for retail

Following the farmer's market retailers and restaurants are likely to be the best choices for selling your items. The items are not in inventory, and the price per unit is adequate.

A business that sells directly to its customers and then connects them to their customers is considered to be a retail store. This differs from wholesalers who sell in restaurants and in retail stores that create two connections between the business with its patrons. Tests have revealed that restaurants and retail stores share similar sales and markets; They likely have retail outlets on their own and they both have the same costs.

If you're considering visiting retail stores or eating places, the primary aspect to take into account is the delivery. For ease of use, it's advised to establish an established delivery schedule as well as extra time for delivery. Also, calculate the distance prior to stepping into the location of a business, and should it be necessary, charge charges for delivery.

Restaurants and stores typically have prices for various items that can vary depending on the season. utilize your production capacity that's available year-round, to your advantage in your deliberations.

Here are some tips to sell to restaurants.

A consistent supply of foods is crucial. The majority of restaurants offer a consistent menu all year round, that can be a major problem in the event that the supply of items like lettuce is restricted for a period of about an entire week, which forces the restaurant to seek a different source. As an aquaponics producer you can take advantage of giving them supplies all year. Also, it is advisable to meet the delivery agreement.

You are likely to offer them a complete menu. Thus, providing consistent products is a must. The majority the sales you make will repeat frequently but occasionally, a brand novel product might be needed.

As you advance in business, you should promote your farm and brand. Good chefs seek out great farmers and are prepared to maintain a relationship for the rest of their lives with them, in order to be the best farmer.

Here are some tips to sell in retail stores

It is recommended to always be multi-faceted and is the best option. In contrast to restaurants that make preferences on menus that are already established constant change in how they decide is an enormous benefit for retail stores in a variety of ways. It is possible to go into this market only when retail stores are your main source of revenue and you require a large number of stores.

Wholesale distributors

The people who work in this field are intermediaries between restaurants and retail stores and, naturally farmers. They do not have any concerns regarding the production of the products or selling those products to the end-users, who are also consumers. They're an additional component of the chain of supply.

If you sell to wholesalers, you may make less money per unit, as well as less. However, the majority of wholesalers are able to take as much products as they want, typically on pallets, but get some of the items from you. When compared to other wholesalers, it is the smallest amount and, therefore it is the lowest benefit gained.

Conclusion

It is important to know how to regulate the temperature of your water to allow your fish to flourish. It is essential to understand how to monitor and regulate pH, ammonialevels, the levels of nitrite and nitrate for the fish to thrive. You must know the species of fish that work best with what plants, and what kind of produce you can cultivate depending on the climate, location and the design of your system.

You must understand the significance of every piece of equipment and how they impact the equilibrium of the aquaponic ecosystem. It is essential to determine the most suitable crops to plant, and figure the ones that make the highest economic value to develop. It is also important to know how to deal with unanticipated and unexpected pests, and ways to eliminate these without putting stress on the fish and the plants.

There are a myriad of things that could go wrong when the process of establishing, running and maintaining your aquaponics farming farm. If everything is in order however even a small aquaponics farm could provide healthy fish and vegetables for families for decades and decades to be. I hope you've gained a few insights about aquaponics, and that I could spark your interest in this eco-friendly urban farming technique. There's still plenty of things to know about aquaponics and there is a lot of research currently being conducted.

www.ingramcontent.com/pod-product-compliance
Lightning Source LLC
Chambersburg PA
CBHW071217210326
41597CB00016B/1847